T0398893

On Display

Recent Titles in
COMPUTATIONAL SOCIAL SCIENCE

Edited by Chris Bail

On Display: Instagram, the Self, and the City
John D. Boy and Justus Uitermark

On Display

Instagram, the Self, and the City

JOHN D. BOY AND JUSTUS UITERMARK

OXFORD
UNIVERSITY PRESS

Oxford University Press is a department of the University of Oxford. It furthers the University's objective of excellence in research, scholarship, and education by publishing worldwide. Oxford is a registered trade mark of Oxford University Press in the UK and certain other countries.

Published in the United States of America by Oxford University Press
198 Madison Avenue, New York, NY 10016, United States of America.

Library of Congress Cataloging-in-Publication Data
Names: Boy, John D., author. | Uitermark, Justus, author.
Title: On display : Instagram, the self, and the city / John D. Boy, Justus Uitermark.
Description: New York, NY : Oxford University Press, [2024] |
Series: Computational social science | Includes bibliographical references and index.
Identifiers: LCCN 2023033303 (print) | LCCN 2023033304 (ebook) |
ISBN 9780197629444 (paperback) | ISBN 9780197629437 (hardback) |
ISBN 9780197629468 (epub)
Subjects: LCSH: Instagram (Electronic resource) | Online social networks—Psychological aspects. | Photographs—Psychological aspects. | Social status. | Self. | Cities and towns in mass media. | Social media and society.
Classification: LCC HM742 .B69 2024 (print) | LCC HM742 (ebook) |
DDC 302.3028501/9—dc23/eng/20230902
LC record available at https://lccn.loc.gov/2023033303
LC ebook record available at https://lccn.loc.gov/2023033304

DOI: 10.1093/oso/9780197629437.001.0001

For Bahar and Corinna

Contents

Acknowledgments

This book would not have seen the light of day without generous input from our students, research participants, and colleagues. We are particularly indebted to Irene Bronsvoort, Marije Peute, and Laura Savolainen, who conducted many of the interviews on which this book is based, co-authored articles that we draw upon here, and shaped our thinking about Instagram.

Many Instagram users shared their experiences and expertise with us over the years, telling us about how Instagram, the self, and the city come together in their lives. Some went as far as volunteering to read chapter drafts, stimulating us to sharpen our arguments. Thank you for allowing us into your lives and contributing your insights.

Our collaboration began thanks to a joint research project with David E. J. Herbert that was generously funded by the Norwegian Research Council. We are grateful to David for numerous discussions over the years. Through the project our work also benefited from the contributions of Alexis Creten, Stefan Fisher-Høyrem, Janna Egholm Hansen, and Pål Steinar Repstad. We also received funding as part of the European Research Council-funded ODYCCEUS project and we learned a great deal from discussions with the coordinator, Eckehard Olbrich, and other Horizon 2020 consortium members.

We further benefited from conversations with Nick Couldry, Jessie Daniels, Anna Hug, Kim Knott, Giselinde Kuipers, Knut Lundby, Lev Manovich, Thomas Poell, Richard Rogers, Gillian Rose, Sjoerd ter Borg, Petter Törnberg, John Torpey, and Dorien Zandbergen. We were fortunate enough to try out some of this book's ideas in numerous workshops, conferences, and guest lectures. We are grateful to the organizers and attendants. We especially wish to thank Rivke Jaffe and Thomas Poell of the University of Amsterdam's Global Digital Cultures initiative for inviting us to present our work at various stages of development.

Javier Garcia-Bernardo gave us access to an HPC facility that allowed us to perform some of the more computationally complex analyses on which this book is based. We also thank the developers and maintainers of numerous free software packages that made our work possible. Vincent Traag, in particular, helped us apply his community detection techniques that he implemented in a Python package.

Chris Bail gave us crucial encouragement and helped us find the perfect outlet for this book. James Cook, our editor at Oxford University Press, carefully guided the project from proposal to completion. Finally, we are grateful to the anonymous reviewers for their constructive criticisms and helpful suggestions.

1
Introduction

Samantha recalls a time when she took a break from her Instagram feed to care for her terminally ill mother. Thinking back, she calls the period "really, really restful." She didn't simply vanish from Instagram though. Her boyfriend posted the occasional found image matching the beige hues that predominate on Samantha's feed on her behalf. Those among her then roughly nine hundred followers who knew her started wondering what was going on. "Some people were thinking, 'She's having the craziest, most beautiful experience of watching her mother die.'" Needless to say, her ersatz presence did not feature any images of what that experience was really like.

Why was this break from the world's largest image-based social media platform so restful, despite the upheavals in Samantha's private life? The way she tells it, it has to do with a tension she often feels in her relationships. "You used to just be able to go to a friend's house and nobody needed to know," reminisces Samantha, who, at twenty-seven, is old enough to remember a time before every moment was memorialized on social media. Now she finds that she constantly feels conflicted when she's around other people. Should she take this opportunity to post? Or would that come over as gauche? Is she giving her other friends social anxiety? Should she care? These and other nagging questions leave her no quiet moment because the need to reconcile her aspirations with social expectations crept into the crevices of daily life. It all got to be a bit much, hence the welcome reprieve of going on hiatus while her mother lay dying.

On Display. John D. Boy and Justus Uitermark, Oxford University Press. © Oxford University Press 2024.
DOI: 10.1093/oso/9780197629437.003.0001

During that time, she caught herself thinking, "Wow! You can *not* be on Instagram!" But life returned to normal, and her work in brand consulting drew her back. Not just that, she even set out to gain followers to grow her "perceived influence," an important asset in her line of work. She let herself become embroiled in Instagram's relentless social dynamics once again. As she was building her online presence, she occasionally also wanted to let her political commitments shine through. As an Amsterdam-based American expat, she took a strong interest in her home country's politics. During our interview, she spoke eloquently about her concern that intersecting power structures in the United States perpetuate the country's legacy of patriarchal and colonial violence. But doubts kept nagging her whenever she tried to express these convictions through the images and captions she posted online. "Is this political? I don't know that it is. This might be a performance—'Hey, look at me! I'm political and I know things.'" Mentioning her Latinx heritage in the caption of a post condemning the internment of migrant children along the southern border didn't feel powerful to her, but indulgent. She removed that post. In fact, no expression of her political commitment remains on her profile. Through all her struggles with the platform, she has settled on a "safe" persona exhibiting professional success, quirky humor, and an Instagram-typical aesthetic.

Sticking to the script is not just a matter of managing the impression she makes on others. It has come to profoundly affect her sense of self. After all, can she truly claim to be a feminist if she doesn't act on the convictions she purports to hold? Can she really separate out the good-natured individual she plays for Instagram from her everyday personality? It's unsettling to think about because she feels that the answer to both questions is likely "no." In no small part, Instagram has made her who she is today.

Sticking to the script as a way of managing struggles with Instagram has become a major cultural phenomenon of our time. Tensions don't just beset individuals like Samantha, but they come to the fore in organizations and businesses as well, as they ponder what they want to represent online. Deborah found herself at the center of such tensions. As a content creator working for Amsterdam's Eye Film Museum, she wants to make the Museum's social media feeds look appealing. In order to reach new market segments, the Museum adopted a social media strategy of creating "likable" content in lieu of "high-brow" messages. That meant, for instance, showing bright colors, the Museum's iconic exterior, or accessible images like portraits of Scarlet Johansson or posters of well-loved Scorsese movies on its Instagram account rather than old archival material. But, she told us, "the Eye is really persistent about wanting to hold on to the information factor, and that makes it tricky to create nice posts." The Museum's core mission to document and show Dutch film history proved difficult to translate into an appealing social media strategy. Instead, the organization embraced Instagram's dominant visual idiom, what the media scholar Lev Manovich (2017) has called "Instagrammism," which allowed the Museum to attract followers and foster engagement. This also led to tensions within the organization, with some of Deborah's colleagues bemoaning a loss of historical awareness. Deborah understands these concerns, but she sees Instagram as unavoidable. The only alternative is irrelevance.

Social media in general, and Instagram in particular, have a reputation for shallowness; however, the sort of self-presentation they demand compels users to do soul-searching and confronts them with profound dilemmas. What do we want to show of ourselves? Who are we? What do we want to be? While it is easy to place blame on individuals or organizations for manipulating their image in the eyes of the world with the help of social media, there is an ineluctable *social* dimension to these personal and aesthetic choices—we don't simply "use" social media, but we change ourselves through them. *On Display* is a book about how people remake their worlds through social media. We explore this process through a series of studies relating to Instagram situated in our hometown of

Amsterdam. In 2018, Instagram hit the milestone of one billion users worldwide (Stevenson 2018). Growth has continued apace; an October 2022 report stated that the platform had reached two billion monthly active users (Barinka 2022). Instagram is also among the most widely used social media platforms in the Netherlands, with an active user base of 7.8 million in 2023. Among cohorts younger than thirty-five, more than half use Instagram daily, and recently growth has also picked up among older users (Hoekstra, Jonker, and van der Veer 2023). That so many people spend so much time on Instagram affects them personally, but also shapes what sorts of relations, subcultures, and spaces take shape—or fall apart—more broadly. As Instagram is woven into the fabric of everyday life, how do people's sense of self, their relations to others, and their environments change?

Looking for Conflict on Instagram

While we are convinced that these are indeed urgent questions, we must admit that we arrived at them via a circuitous route. This book has its origins in a research project on how digital media reshape cultural conflict that ran from 2015 through 2018.[1] When we started planning the research that laid the foundation for this book, we were interested in discovering how local conflicts scale up, and who was being empowered or held back in the process. As a possible way of answering that question, we discussed picking a cultural conflict and examining where it plays out and how it scales up—or not. In the inaugural meeting of our research team, we discussed a range of cultural conflicts subject to public debate at the time involving the hijab, hipsters, mosque construction, Spanish bullfighting, tourists, the Dutch character Black Pete, and more. Surely we could study these flash points and conflicts online. We would simply apply the standard recipe for computational research on cultural conflicts—identify hashtags associated with the conflict on Twitter, harvest the tweets mentioning the hashtags, discover that there are different groups of Twitter users who struggle to define what the conflict is about, and identify one or a set of factors accounting for how the conflict played out—but we increasingly felt that would amount to projecting preconceived notions of what constitutes a "cultural conflict." We feared that our findings would reflect rather than inform our understanding of our cultural predicament.

We began contemplating what we described at the time as an "agnostic approach." While acknowledging that all approaches, even the most radically open and inductive, are rooted in notions of what counts as relevant data, we wanted to have the data speak to us to move beyond stereotypical and preconceived notions of what a cultural conflict entails. Only after getting a sense of the wide range of local conflicts that social media users engage in, would we examine how some scale up while others do not.

While we pursued the tried-and-true strategy of collecting information from Twitter, we also became aware of another social media platform called Instagram. We had little familiarity with the platform before then. One of us had had an account early on but closed it again after he grew convinced that his photography skills were not up to snuff, while the other had never even installed the app. A visual medium that's especially popular among younger generations, what interested us most about Instagram were its geo-locative features. More than on Twitter or any other popular platform, Instagram users are encouraged to geotag their posts; that is, they associate the content they produce with places. We figured that Instagram is the ideal medium to study cultural conflicts agnostically. We would identify posts in a specific area with first-person accounts of grievances—people speaking out about traffic congestion, immigrants, housing prices, racism, unpaid overtime, and so on—and then examine how such individual grievances feed from and into broader conflicts. Casting a wide net was possible thanks to the possibilities Instagram then had (and has since restricted) of gathering data through a specialized interface. We began collecting thousands of Instagram posts every day from the cities we were interested in—including Amsterdam—as well as all likes and comments on those posts, hoping that social media data would allow us to study social life as it unfolded. Social scientists had become mesmerized by the possibilities opened up by the "data deluge" of our age for the fine-grained study of human behavior, and we had similarly high hopes for the study of digital trace data.

However, what we saw was not what we had anticipated. Rather than seeing a reflection of social life as it unfolded, we saw a curious inflection of life in the city, refashioned according to a peculiar aesthetic. We found that what Instagram users see as they scroll through their feeds, what they post, and how they use the platform to navigate social and urban worlds are all marked by this prevailing aesthetic. Instagram posts capture moments—moments set apart by their refined beauty and good vibes. They are rarely spectacular, but rather capture an individual's street-level view of daily urban life, lovingly arranged possessions, or convivial occasions. In one picture we found a large group of cyclists waiting for a green light at an intersection; in another, a Jeff Buckley record sleeve artfully propped up atop a record player; in a third, we saw young women and men dressed for a special occasion, smiling and enjoying drinks together. And, of course, we also found selfies, latte art, and beautifully plated avocado toast. In the process of reassembling their life-world in this manner, the everyday is relentlessly aestheticized to the point that it never appears as the merely ordinary or mundane. Looking through a stream of Instagram posts, we see a seemingly interminable series of peak moments.

When we recount the story of how we came to study Instagram, our audiences, and especially students, are often at a loss: "Why would you study *Instagram* if you were interested in cultural conflict? How naïve! *Of course* you would only see people showing off the good sides of their lives." We understand the response. Perhaps we took our agnostic approach a bit too far when we naïvely decided to study a platform with which we had little familiarity. And yet, while there are certainly downsides to studying alien cultures and practices, our ignorance bore some advantages, too. What was trivial for our students was a puzzle to us: we wanted to understand how this particular symbolic universe came about and how it refashions conflicts, cities, and everyday life. The sociologist Deana Rohlinger (2019) invokes the image of fish in water who cannot recognize the fluid their lives depend on because it's simply their reality. "We swim in a technological world, yet like fish, we rarely think about how new media potentially change the ways in which we interact with one another or shape how we live our lives" (Rohlinger 2019, 3). To be honest, we never got any better at Instagram, even after years of research. We're not writing as proficient users, and we certainly don't have much advice to give to aspiring influencers. Unlike Crystal Abidin, the foremost ethnographer of Instagram, we do not immerse ourselves in the symbolic universe we study (Abidin 2018, 2020). We cannot lay claim to first-hand knowledge of the workings of internet fame. We also do not devote much attention to the specific cultural vernacular that defines Instagram as a platform (see Leaver, Highfield, and Abidin 2020). While we acknowledge and study Instagram's particularities, this is not a book about this platform's unique culture. And unlike scholars of science and technology, we do not have the ambition to delve deep into Instagram's interface or algorithms. There is much to learn from such research, but it is not the kind of study we did.

Relational Sociology

So, how *did* we study Instagram? Our approach is premised on the conviction that social structures and individual sensibilities hang together—what we feel, think, want, and do is inseparable from how we are connected to one another. This means that Instagram itself is not the object of analysis of this book, but rather the relations between the platform and people and places forged in the practice of everyday life. If we want to understand social media platforms like Instagram and how they change social worlds, we believe that we must study them not on their own terms, as digital networks of communication and sharing. Instead, we must conceive of them primarily as *stages* where people define and negotiate their place in the social world. Wanting to put this conception on a firm conceptual basis prompted us to trawl what our discipline of sociology has to offer to make sense of what we came to see as the defining mark of social media: generalized status competition. Two relational sociologists, in particular, guided our thinking: Pierre Bourdieu and Norbert Elias.

We view Instagram as a field in the sense of Bourdieu. Instagram is a *symbolic universe* onto itself. It has its own aesthetics and vernacular that are difficult to comprehend and navigate for the uninitiated. Like any field, Instagram has field-specific rewards that are meaningless, or even obscene, to outsiders but highly valuable to those who are invested in the platform. Followers, likes, and favorable comments represent symbolic capital that bestow status on those who participate in the field. These field-specific rewards are distributed unevenly across users, with some being cast in central and almost sacred roles and others relegated to playing a supporting act. The more invested people are in Instagram, the more they are enthralled by the field's *illusio*; that is, the conviction that the field-specific rewards are worth playing for.

Conceptualizing Instagram as a field allows us to steer a course between, on the one hand, seeing Instagram as an independent entity and, on the other, seeing it as merely a reflection of society at large. Instagram is a reflection in that its symbolic hierarchy is strongly shaped by inequalities within the broader society. Users who bring resources and connections to the platform generally fare better than those who do not. But Instagram is not just a reflection; it mediates relations. People construe their selves and their relations in creative ways. The fact that what is outside of Instagram does not determine what is on it is what makes the game interesting and worth playing. Moreover, the rewards Instagram offers are valuable beyond the platform. People may do well on Instagram because they have many friends or because they are good fashion designers, but they may also make more friends or gain recognition as fashion designers because they do well on Instagram. The field metaphor captures the *relative autonomy* of Instagram, the specificity of its symbolic universe as well as its embeddedness within broader social relations. Viewing Instagram as a field means we are interested in understanding how inequalities in this symbolic universe are structured and how they, in turn, shape inequalities outside of the platform.

While we take from Bourdieu the idea of studying Instagram as a symbolic universe, we use Elias to better understand what kind of field it is and how people navigate it.[2] Whereas Bourdieu sometimes makes it seem as if people rationally optimize their lives in pursuit of status, Elias directs our attention to the mixed feelings and inner conflicts people experience. Displaying status on Instagram is not as straightforward as it may seem—it raises questions about who you are, what you want to be, and which people you want to relate to or dissociate from. It is not just an individual expression, but it involves estimating others' expectations and anticipating their responses. Elias helps us to explore the relationship between social structures and individual sensibilities and to unearth the conflicts—both *between* people and *within* them—that lie behind the mundane pictures that populate Instagram feeds.

Following Elias, social media compel users to see themselves through the eyes of others. As they become embedded in networks that span different social circles and settings, users must reckon with a growing number of groups. The net effect of the densification and extension of chains of interdependencies is to attune people to each other and to bring them into closer alignment. All groups of Instagram users we encounter in this book are deeply concerned with the image they convey, and they devote much of their energy pondering how their attires, expressions, or statements are perceived by proximate or remote others. While many researchers emphasize how social media fosters polarization and fragmentation, our perspective and data led us in a different direction: we view social media as reflective and supportive of social integration. Like Elias before us, we do not consider integration to be an inherently good thing. Being connected to many others in myriad ways can result in stresses and strains, especially when such connections are forged within a context of precarity and competition. Those with whom we are connected may prey on us, not stand in solidarity with us.

Building on classical sociologists like Bourdieu and Elias may raise eyebrows. Why use the work of two long-dead, white, male, European sociologists when there has been a proliferation of work on digital cultures by authors with a wide range of perspectives, backgrounds, and cases? One reason we find it helpful to call on these authors is that they unsettle a propensity to see only "newness" and instead help see continuities in how social relations and the sense of self are produced. Instagram and other social media platforms are sites of new sensibilities, aesthetics, and social norms, but they are also sites where perennial themes of human social relations—inequality, integration, power—play out. We use insights from classical sociology to situate Instagram in long-term processes and to view the social relations that take shape on the platform as specific renditions of such classic themes.

Another reason for using these two classic sociologists is that their work aligns with contributions by scholars like Alice Marwick (2013) and Brooke Erin Duffy (2017), who emphasize the importance of status to understanding online sociality. As we explain in greater detail in the following chapter, these authors suggest a paradigm shift by moving away from analyzing social media as sites for deliberation toward understanding them as stages where status is enacted and negotiated. These works grasp at the nature of emerging social roles and hierarchies of status in the context of contemporary gender relations, economic imperatives, and intersecting systems of oppression. These more recent works further show how digital technologies are implicated in the construction of status hierarchies. Alice Marwick's *Status Update*, in particular, demonstrates how the architecture of social media reflects the contradiction between nominal equality and actual hierarchy in neoliberal society.[3] Social media allow for horizontal relations but also facilitate inequalities between leaders and followers; they are made for spontaneous social interaction between friends but also encourage strategic maneuvering to rise in the hierarchy. Marwick observed these contradictions of incipient digital capitalism in the Bay Area technology scene around the year 2010, but they have since diffused widely. "Self-branding" is no longer practiced solely by the aspiring technology entrepreneurs who were the designers and early adopters of digital platforms—children now learn the technique when they take their first steps online, and professionals in many domains must practice it to get ahead. Marwick warned that "there are consequences for moving our social lives into realms that are so focused on the free market" (2013, 19). We take stock of such consequences, studying how people's relations, environments, and subjectivities change as they are mediated by digital platforms.

Methods

Although we focus on Instagram and the relations and sensibilities formed through this platform, we consistently *situate* Instagram within the social and geographic environment of Amsterdam. Where media scholars, psychologists, and communications scholars often try to isolate specific media cultures or effects of media use, we start off from the premise that Instagram is embedded within wider sets of relations and woven into the fabric of everyday life (Baym 2015). Instagram doesn't have agency of its own, nor is it simply a reflection of its environment. Rather, it is a field that *mediates* social relations and our sense of self. Social media are not just added on top of already existing relations but reconfigure and refract them. They are *ecological* rather than additive, in Neil Postman's words (2010, 5).

While Postman used ecology as a metaphor to bring to the fore the profound and pervasive effects of media technologies, the other side of the coin is that social media do not act alone and never determine what happens—they are always only a part of what is going on. For instance, when we study the impact of Instagram on urban change, we should view the platform as a mediator of endemic processes like gentrification or segregation rather than as a *deus ex machina*. Similarly, if we want to understand how the rise of Instagram shapes feminism, we need to situate the platform and its users in long-term historical changes in gender relations and successive waves of social movement activism. We can only understand social media if we look beyond them to see the wider processes and environments of which they are a part. Just as Nick Couldry (2012) argues against a media-centric view in favor of understanding media *practices*, we need to avoid a platform-centric view and consider the broader sets of relations in which Instagram is embedded. Our general strategy, then, is to use granular qualitative and computational data to provide a detailed account of the social relations and sensibilities of Instagram's users while sketching in broad brushes the historical processes and geographic environments in which these relations and sensibilities are situated.

To understand the structure of social relations on Instagram, we use computational methods, especially network analysis. Our computational analyses rely in part on a unique dataset of 709,348 posts and 34.4 million interactions that we collected between December 2015 and June 2016, just before Instagram restricted access to such data. Using this dataset, we can study how Instagram users in Amsterdam self-organize into distinct though interlocking subgroups, chart emerging hierarchies among users, map where they post, and see what they post about.

To get at the subjective dimension of Instagram, we—together with our research team—conducted interviews with eighty-five interlocutors between 2015 and 2020, with a handful agreeing to be reinterviewed after several years to reflect on changes and continuities in their Instagram use over time. Understanding the interface between Amsterdam and Instagram to be our field site, we chose multiple entry points (see Burrell 2009). Using our database, we identified high-centrality users, both for the city as a whole and for specific subgroups and neighborhoods, as well as establishments that were often tagged in Instagram posts. We also interviewed marketing and public relations agencies shaping the image of highly visible locations. In addition, we made a targeted effort to contact users from groups that would otherwise not be represented in our data but who might serve to "inconvenience" the picture we were getting of how, why, and where Instagram tends to be used (Duneier 2011). This included men, residents from working-class neighborhoods, and older users. Similarly, we visited locations that are conspicuously absent from Instagram to understand the reasons for their invisibility. Our sample includes a few interviewees whose presence on the platform is decisive for their professional activities and who might be described as "influencers," while others are casual users who only use the platform occasionally. The vast majority are what we might call intensive users: their lives do not revolve around Instagram, but it is important to them, and they spend a lot of time browsing their feeds and posting stories and pictures. We make no pretense that the sample we generated in this manner is representative, but we believe it has enabled us to get a fair overview of how Instagram is used, anticipated, or avoided in everyday situations by a wide range of urban dwellers.

Although we adapted our questions over time, we always took care not to have Instagram become too "obvious" to us. In interviews, we would ask Instagram users seemingly trivial questions. What do you see when you look over your own feed and those of others? How do you decide to post? How do you choose to follow certain accounts? The interviewees would become aware of what they already knew as we tapped their tacit knowledge about the platform and the sorts of practices that do or do not belong there. Often, the interviews would serve a therapeutic purpose for participants—they would talk about the social relations in which they were enmeshed and the conflicted feelings they had about relating to others through Instagram. Such conversations were, of course, never only or even mostly about Instagram—they are also about broader social relations and an evolving sense of self. Samantha's experience with the platform was shaped, for instance, by her engagement with intersectional feminism and her mother's terminal illness.

Amsterdam

A city of about nine hundred thousand, Amsterdam is the cultural capital of the Netherlands. Aside from being a major draw for tourists—well over sixteen million in a regular year—Amsterdam has a diverse population. Around one-quarter of the city's inhabitants are foreign-born, and well over one-half have non-Dutch origins. While rising housing prices and gentrification have made access to the city more difficult, Amsterdam's progressive history of social housing provision means that proportionally less of the working-class population has been displaced by these processes than in other major European cities. Even so, the city's public life is shaped by the many creative professionals who call Amsterdam home, and various establishments for upscale consumption are a pervasive presence. Urban geographers Boterman and van Gent (2023, 162) characterize these transformations as a form of "soft gentrification" because of its reliance on cultural, rather than coercive, means. Amsterdam's urban landscape is characteristic and especially its canal houses are recognized the world over, but Amsterdam lacks any immediately recognizable landmarks analogous to the Eiffel Tower. This is the environment in which many of the people who feature in this book live, work, and play.

Our focus on a particular city is unusual for media studies, but also might raise eyebrows in urban studies. Recent theorizing has argued that the proper object of study for urban studies is not the entity referred to as "the city" but the *process* of urbanization (e.g., Brenner and Schmid 2015). This literature cautions against "methodological cityism," arguing that urbanization is a process that involves inner cities as much as hinterlands, and inter-city as much as intra-city connections. In this perspective, "the city" is, at best, a specific expression of this larger process and, at worst, an ideological *idée fixe* that blocks us from grasping the urbanization process (Wachsmuth 2014).

This critique is particularly relevant in a context where wide swaths of everyday experience are digitally mediated, including our relation to place (Halegoua 2020). Media theorists have argued that social life is not just mediated, but *mediatized*—that is, molded by the logics of media. Given how deeply enmeshed social life has become with mediated processes (Couldry and Hepp 2018), "Amsterdam" is not as straightforward a geographic referent as it may seem as people increasingly experience places not only in situ but also remotely. Even when they are within the municipal boundaries, they navigate the city using digital technologies produced by global corporations, view posts produced elsewhere, and interact with distant others. Just as urbanization is a planetary process, so is digitally powered mediatization. Extracting an arbitrarily defined slice out of global networks—those relations and people contained within the boundaries of Amsterdam—risks missing something essential about mediatized cities, namely that their experience and production extends across their boundaries. For pragmatic reasons, we used the boundaries of the municipality to delimit our data collection, but this method of sampling excludes the many interactions crossing Amsterdam's municipal borders and arbitrarily cuts off the city from its surroundings.

How to deal with this conundrum? One way is to use the fine-grained information from interviews and general insights from the literature to contextualize findings on Instagram interactions and geotags in Amsterdam. While our focus is on Amsterdam, our fieldwork followed interviewees beyond the city boundaries. Focusing on Amsterdam is for us a way to *situate* our research, making it possible to study how Instagram use is mediated by geographically and historically specific relationships.

Another way to avoid reifying the city is to focus on the uneven production of space *within* Amsterdam. As Neil Brenner and colleagues argue, planetary urbanization involves both explosion and implosion, creating highly uneven landscapes. We observe something similar in our study of Instagram in Amsterdam: while users and places are part of global networks, they focus their attention on specific places within the city. This unevenness is stark when we map geotagged posts from Amsterdam. They are heavily concentrated in the historical center and gentrifying districts, and looking within neighborhoods, we find that some places stand out while others are nearly invisible. Grand parks, hip bars, and historical buildings figure prominently while supermarkets, high roads, and residential blocks are absent.

One important task for us, then, is to understand how some places and people are elevated while others are pushed to the background. What is it that makes specific places in the city so important as stages and markers for Instagram? We argue that the practices of distinction and the processes of differentiation that theorists such as Georg Simmel (2021) associated with the modern metropolis now take place in an urban environment that is partially constituted through digital media. Places within the city allow for displays of status on Instagram, and these displays, in turn, shape the constitution of place. We are interested precisely in the space that emerges at the interface of cities and digital platforms. Acknowledging that the grounding of our research in Amsterdam only offers us insights into these general processes from one particular place, we nevertheless chose this focus because it allows us to offer a contextualized and up-close account of Instagram's role in mediating how people find their way in the city and society at large.

Integration, Inequality, Conformity

While in retrospect it may seem hopelessly naïve that we came to Instagram to study cultural and political conflict, we had good reasons. There is a venerable literature that views social media as a "networked public sphere" in which citizens and social movements have unprecedented opportunities to voice their concerns and organize for social change (e.g., Castells 2012; Benkler et al. 2015). Although this idea of a networked public sphere fits particular types of cases well, not much of what we saw on the platform or heard from our interviewees made sense from this perspective. Expressions of criticism were the exception, not the rule. Organizing for social change happened, but rarely. When we specifically sought out activists, they told us that they struggled to use the platform. They felt that Instagram offered little scope for activism because it encourages individualism and is for messages that convey "good vibes" and pictures that are aesthetically pleasing.

If our understanding of social media—shaped by a large literature—fit a large and influential platform like Instagram so poorly, then surely there is a need for reconsidering established notions of what social media are and do. Instagram came to serve as a "critical case" (Flyvbjerg 2006) to interrogate some widely accepted notions about social media. Rather than rejecting established ideas of what defines social media, we use Instagram to highlight features, processes, and effects that might easily be overlooked if we restrict ourselves to the favorites of social media researchers (Facebook and especially Twitter).[4] We wanted to understand Instagram to help us rethink social media.

As our research on Instagram prompted us to rethink our premises, we came to view social media as vehicles for the display of status rather than the exchange of arguments. As we explain in more detail in the following chapter, the absolutist court of early modern Europe described by Norbert Elias might be a better metaphor for social media than the bourgeois public sphere of the early nineteenth century described by Jürgen Habermas. In court society, nobles and other courtiers engage in gossip, don glamorous outfits, or play up to the king to improve their position. People act out their position but also aspire to move upward, emulating the styles, poses, and garments of those who are above them. Many of the seemingly awkward habits of Instagram users become intelligible when we stop understanding them as genuine expressions of individuality or symptoms of pathologies and begin seeing them as markers of social status and aspiration. When someone posts a skillfully taken picture of latte art, they are not just capturing a moment in their lives. They are also applying their knowledge of Instagram tropes to declare they are in a class of people who are cognizant of the finer products of today's refined metropolitan culture.

Seen from this perspective, Instagram enmeshes users in extensive and heterogeneous networks in which they are enticed to affirm dominant norms of beauty and success. It is not that Instagram is always or necessarily used to affirm dominant norms, but our argument is that this is the default. We develop this argument in three steps. First, we show that Instagram networks are *integrated*: rather than pulling people apart, they bring them together. Second, Instagram networks are *unequal*: rather than bringing people together in egalitarian networks, they insert them into systems of stratified rank. Third, Instagram networks promote *conformity* because in their integrated yet uneven symbolic universe, deviation is minute rather than radical.

Instagram Networks Are Integrated

A central argument of this book is that Instagram networks are integrated, rather than segregated. Here, our argument cuts against the grain of received wisdom and general sentiment. Many scholars have taken issue with the idea that social media serve to bridge differences and bring different groups of people together. An academic industry has grown around the idea that social media are sites of disintegration, using notions like "echo chambers," "balkanization," or "bubbles" to convey that the space for resolving our collective problems through debate is rapidly disappearing. Much of the work in this domain is based on Twitter research, simulated social worlds, or a combination of both. The interdisciplinary field studying "opinion dynamics," for instance, has produced a series of models that vary in their details but generally show how homophily—the tendency to form bonds with those who are like us—results in local consensus but global polarization. Empirical research on political debates on social media, typically Twitter, is then used to show that, indeed, partisan users tend to mostly retweet or follow others they agree with.

The issue with this line of argument is not that it is wrong, but that it is one-sided. When they construct their models, opinion dynamics researchers typically write rules expressly designed to accentuate polarization. When they look at empirical reality, they select the settings most likely to affirm the view that social media promotes polarization. Typically, they look at debates on political topics by partisans on Twitter—a thin slice of users on a particular platform, and by far not the largest one. This way of working helps to better identify the mechanisms that might produce polarization, but it is unlikely to provide insight into countervailing mechanisms or to suggest new angles for understanding how social media shape social conflict. When we first looked at our Instagram data, we attempted to walk the same path. We assumed that people would self-organize into homogeneous groups. We further assumed, again faithfully following the literature, that these groups would not only have their own spaces online but also in cities (Boy and Uitermark 2016, 2017). That's indeed true, but there are also other forces at play. We are now convinced that these forces are too important to be disregarded as aberrant noise.

The mishmash of connections we found among Instagram users defies any simple characterization in terms of fragmentation, let alone polarization. Yes, people organize into homogeneous groups, but typically not just one: they sort according to taste, ethnicity, location, political preference, profession, and so on. The aggregate result is not a space neatly divided, but a mishmash of interrelated clusters. These patterns were so salient that we felt we had to consider that integration, not segregation, might be a hallmark of Instagram. What does it mean to conceive of Instagram in this way? It's not just a minor quibble with existing analyses; instead, it has far-reaching implications. Seeing Instagram as internally differentiated but integrated allows us to examine the formidable processes pushing toward conformity operative on the platform. In a world of mutually closed-off bubbles, highly diverging forms of expression can exist in their respective cultural environments. But when connections span different social groups, we must carefully attune our expressions to more widely shared standards. When we post to Instagram, we typically consider multiple audiences: not just one group of close friends, but multiple circles of friends, and not just friends, but also classmates, colleagues, family members, distant acquaintances, and, at times, even strangers. To avoid offense to any one of these groups, users typically default to expressions that are non-confrontational. That Instagram feeds occasionally appear repetitive and conformist is not because users are bland, but because they conform to many different expectations. In such integrated hierarchies, strategies of distinction operate in subtle ways.

Instagram Reflects and Reinforces Inequality

Instagram networks are highly unequal. This will not come as a surprise to contemporary readers, but it is important to bear in mind that an earlier generation of researchers and users considered the internet in general, and social media in particular, as incubators of horizontal and egalitarian relations. The sociologist Manuel Castells (2012), to mention one prominent example, considered "horizontality" a defining feature of social media networks. Proliferating research in network science has, however, demonstrated that social media networks tend to have highly unequal degree distributions (González-Bailón and Wang 2016; Barberá et al. 2015). That means that a minority of nodes accounts for the majority of connections—a feature that social media networks share with many other kinds of self-organized networks (Barabási 2002). We extend this work by prosaically confirming that Instagram networks are indeed highly unequal. This is true no matter how we cut them—whether we look at networks at the level of the city or the neighborhood, or whether we look at the population as a whole or specific clusters within it—time and again we find that same, highly unequal pattern repeated.

Then we take another step. Most computational research on social media networks is based only on platform data, so it effectively treats platforms as autonomous universes. Our research advances scholarship that examines how digital inequalities are structured by and feed back into broader patterns of inequality. Most Amsterdammers have internet access, so there is not much of a "digital divide" in the classical sense to speak of. What remains are inequalities in terms of how digital media are used and who produces content (Schradie 2011; van Deursen and van Dijk 2014)—and this gap coincides with socio-spatial inequalities (see also Lane 2018; Lane and Marler 2020). We find that residents who are white, affluent, upwardly mobile, and healthy have an outsize impact on how the city is represented on Instagram. The platform is one of the preferred sites where affluent urban dwellers put their tentative renderings of the ideal city on display. The close-ups of avocado toast or coffee cups and the group pictures of people enjoying craft beer and concerts are not just personal mementos but convey idealized ways of being in the world to followers. In Chapters 5 and 6, we show that, while some establishments and subcultures are elevated in these displays of status, other establishments and subcultures, especially those on the margin, are blotted out. For the aspirational class, to use the urbanist Elizabeth Currid-Halkett's (2017) phrase, Instagram becomes a site of prefiguration. Instagram shapes the use of space by drawing attention to some places rather than others, and by demonstrating how to consume space aspirationally.

Instagram Engenders Minute Deviations

Now we return to the question that animated our interest in the platform in the first place, the question of cultural conflict. Does Instagram figure into cultural conflicts, and if so, how? Having established that social relations on Instagram are highly uneven and generate pressures toward conformity, we conclude that Instagram is generally not conducive to resistance. The omnipresence of Instagram and of networked devices extends the gaze of the mainstream. Activists, radicals, and others who deviate from the norm must consider that they may be on display at all times. This causes many to be mindful of the potential to become visible in ways they cannot control.

This does not mean, however, that conformity is all there is to Instagram. Many Instagram users want to raise issues they care deeply about and challenge ingrained power structures. In Chapter 6, we meet Aisha Tahiri, an Amsterdam-based activist and entrepreneur who is fiercely and vocally committed to fighting racism and inequality. As an activist, she is deeply concerned about the fate of immigrant entrepreneurs under threat of displacement, but as a consultant she harnesses the forces of gentrification. She explains that many of the gentrifiers coming into her neighborhood have "Instagram vision" and only register new establishments while failing to see what immigrant entrepreneurs have to offer. Her solution is to help immigrant entrepreneurs become "Insta-proof" by redesigning their storefronts and signage; crafting appealing images; and rebranding traditional foodstuffs, like chai or bulgur, as "superfoods." Radical convictions are rendered into minute adjustments.

We tackle the question of how Instagram figures into movements for progressive change directly in Chapter 4. For feminists who are sex-positive, body positive, or who feel that radiating confidence and strength is integral to feminist expression, Instagram is an ideal platform. But the platform is much less conducive for posts advocating for global solidarity or alternative understandings of gender norms. More generally, activists are confronted with a catch-22: they must play according to the rules if they want to challenge the rules. One of the women we spoke to felt that women should not be ashamed of their bodies and therefore posts pictures of herself displaying armpit hair. But apart from that detail, her pictures show a conventionally attractive young woman. The example hints at a broader dynamic: the women must pay homage to norms in a big way before they can mount small challenges against them.

Instagram and Interdependencies

The perspective we adopt in this book suggests that Instagram is not just another platform with its own peculiar conventions, but that it is part of a broader development. Social media have served to make the internet more personalized, intimate, and visual, while also making interdependencies more extensive, differentiated, and dense. This is a development that Instagram exemplifies, but not Instagram alone. By the time this book is published, another platform may have taken Instagram's place—but many of the processes and mechanisms we identify here will still apply to what comes next, barring wider revolutionary changes. As we construct our personas and connections through social media, we are compelled to anticipate the views and responses of proximate and distant others.

Seen in this light, Instagram is a peculiar case, but one that, like other platforms, is a stage for status displays, enables self-curated connections, and classifies users and their expressions according to a system of rank. This fateful sociological cocktail is worth understanding more deeply if we want to make sense of our current predicament. This book is meant to help us do precisely that. For that purpose, we introduce some conceptual tools for thinking about social media in the following chapter. The four subsequent chapters look at different aspects of the interplay between social structures and sensibilities, first in the biographies of individual users, and then in the social environment of the city. We conclude by summarizing the main lessons from these chapters with an eye to how they may contribute to public debates about the present and future of humankind's large-scale experiment with social media.

2

Status and Social Media

For as long as there have been social media, commentators have seen them as political phenomena. Early commentators often pointed to the rise of a "networked public sphere," which influential scholars like Manuel Castells (2009) and Yochai Benkler (2007) proposed would empower citizens by enabling them to communicate across national and associational boundaries. Citizens could therefore build community directly and without government interference. This assessment was premised on seeing social media as vehicles of political discourse. Their distributed nature, in particular, was believed to mark an important advance over mass media under corporate control because citizens were no longer beholden to elite gatekeepers.

We are now in a period of backlash against these sorts of utopian hopes. In his *Antisocial Media* (2018), the media scholar Siva Vaidhyanathan presents a sweeping case against Facebook and its properties, detailing the ways the company's business model and algorithms scramble political discourse. Chris Bail (2021) documents how social media's architecture fosters polarization, while Sinan Aral (2020) shows how quickly misinformation can spread. Even before the current backlash, contributors to the debate added a variety of qualifications to the idea that social media constitute a networked public sphere. Zizi Papacharissi (2002) noted that online debates, much like offline ones, are frequently dominated by elites, while Lada Adamic and Natalie Glance (2005) anticipated today's debates over echo chambers by showing how people with different political opinions polarize into distinct groups instead of engaging in debate.

On Display. John D. Boy and Justus Uitermark, Oxford University Press. © Oxford University Press 2024.
DOI: 10.1093/oso/9780197629437.003.0002

These authors have a more pessimistic assessment than Benkler and Castells, but they apply the same standard. Even as they temper optimism, the ideal of the networked public sphere still motivates and frames their research. When scholars recognize that networked spaces don't really live up to the public sphere ideal, they conceptualize them as *deficient* public spheres. The overall idea that online sociality can be meaningfully related to the category of the public sphere is thus accepted, even in the work of those who are most critical of the social and political implications of technological change.

The public sphere prism has helpfully elucidated some specific aspects of social media, but it has also perniciously narrowed our view.[1] By adopting variations on the concept of the public sphere, analysts have failed to grasp and explain what we argue is most essential to social media: the display of status. Boosting one's status is not only about building social relations and gaining recognition, but also about building a personal brand and fulfilling one's aspirations. Writing a decade ago, Alice Marwick's *Status Update* concluded that social media "have enabled the infiltration of neoliberal, market-driven values and ethics into day-to-day relationships with others and even into ways that we, as users of social media, think about ourselves" (2013, 281). Since then, as aspirational repertoires of understanding and performing the self have become generalized (Duffy 2017; Bishop 2022), so have status displays.

Sometimes social media posts take the form of photos with captions, sometimes they are only written, but they are inevitably displays of status in the sense that individuals present themselves for appraisal by others. The "social" in "social media" refers to the modalities for appraisal by others: social media platforms are, regardless of their specific format, designed to let others respond to status displays and, crucially, to value them through "likes," "retweets," or other forms of recognition. The defining quality of social media is that they offer a stage for status displays and provide tools for appraisal and ranking. We do not deny that social media can be harbingers of contestation or deliberation (in fact, as we recalled in the previous chapter, that is what attracted us to the analysis of social media in the first place), but we feel that we can only grasp deliberation or contestation on social media once we acknowledge that these functions are not central for most users most of the time. If we recognize that social media are—not exclusively, but first and foremost—about displays of status, we can pose different sets of questions and grasp what has so far been either ignored altogether or considered as noise.

In this book, we develop this perspective mostly through examples drawn from our research on Instagram, a social media platform that so far has received far less attention from researchers than one might expect based on the size of its user base and its influence on popular culture. Much of our discomfort with understandings of social media stems from our experience that they fit the case of Instagram poorly. While worries over fragmentation are typically voiced in relation to Facebook and, especially, Twitter, Instagram raises a different set of concerns. The budding research literature on Instagram emphasizes that the platform gives ample space to corporate-sponsored influencers to shape tastes and desires (Abidin 2016b) while compelling users to enact idealized selves and hide stress and strains (Duffy and Hund 2015). It is an extension of the culture industry undermining all attempts at symbolic resistance (Manovich 2020). Whereas many studies on Twitter highlight polarization, this literature on Instagram conjures up the image of users connecting in an environment where beauty, wealth, and success are celebrated and aestheticized (see Marwick 2015). While acknowledging Instagram's specificity, we regard the platform as a fruitful, alternative starting point for theorizing social media more broadly.

Instead of imagining social media as harbingers of revolution or vehicles of progressive social change, from this starting point we can recognize the many ways in which social media relates to status politics—sometimes aiding those who mount challenges to entrenched hierarchies, but often facilitating backlash against those who refuse to stay in the place assigned to them by the reigning social order. There is a politics to social media, but that politics cannot be grasped through the Habermasian notions that have encased the debate. Drawing on the work of the German sociologist Norbert Elias, we propose an alternative that we think will serve us better in bringing into focus social processes playing out in digital spaces.

Expressing Status

The work of Norbert Elias provides us with tools to make sense of social media and status politics. Elias is most famous for *The Civilizing Process* (1994), which examines changes in manners and sensibilities between 1250 and 1750. *The Civilizing Process* exemplifies Elias's sociological approach, which forms the basis for our own.[2] Elias's relational sociology analyzes how social relations change and how, in parallel, people's feelings and sensibilities change. In a word, it is about how people are connected and composed (see de Swaan 2001). This approach is productive for understanding networked and media-saturated societies because it helps to situate psychic states at the individual level (our desires, anxieties, and sensibilities) within broader changes in the structure and nature of interdependencies. By conceiving of social media as carriers of interdependence, it also provides a remedy to dualistic perspectives that regard the online as a realm apart from "real life." Another added benefit is that Elias is deeply committed to purging sociological analysis of "wish-images." The public sphere is such a wish-image. Instead of idealizing social media as a public sphere or criticizing social media for its democratic deficiencies, relational sociology wants to understand what sorts of relations form through social media and how people's experiences and sensibilities are constituted.

Elias invites us to situate social media in a long-term historical perspective. Taking that long-term perspective to the extreme, we could say that the prehistory of social media started around seventy thousand years ago when Homo sapiens evolved a language that enabled our species to communicate in great and complex detail. Historians and evolutionary biologists suggest that Homo sapiens' superior language capacity enabled members of the species to outcompete close relatives—including apes and Neanderthals—by allowing cooperation on a much larger scale. Their sophisticated language allowed humans to recognize and develop group symbols. We came to believe and organize in collectives far greater than those predicated on kin relations and face-to-face interactions alone (Elias 1991b). Gossip networks sustain such collectives because they help people to know who to trust and who to shun (Harari 2015). At this point, the management of reputation became vital for individuals and collectives. When people become part of dense and extensive networks, Elias argued, they are compelled to consider how their actions will appear to others with whom they are vicariously connected. *The Civilizing Process* shows how ever greater numbers of people became dependent on each other and, therefore, had to take one another into account. They feared nature and violence less but experienced greater anxiety of losing face. Social survival increasingly revolved around cultivating manners. As they became embroiled in extensive, dense, and differentiated chains of relations, people gradually developed the habit of eating with utensils, having sex out of sight of family members, and refraining from spitting on the floor (Elias 1994). Viewed in this long-term perspective, social media represent one further step in the long and checkered development of the extension and densification of chains of social relations. Social media link people together in networks in which reputation is centrally at stake.

Over time, the vehicles for expressing status have transformed—from paintings to photographs to social media posts. In European court society, oil paintings were an important measure of status. As John Berger (1972) noted, the vast majority of oil paintings are not great works of art. Although some sell for record prices to this day, those are the rare exceptions in an otherwise boring genre. Oil paintings were produced, from the sixteenth century onward, to display the status of the nobles and merchants who had commissioned the paintings. The images typically convey the position of the people in the picture through props and setting: a globe to signal colonial enterprises, fur or gold to express wealth, bucolic landscapes to signify land ownership, and so on. Like photographs taken with portable cameras—or indeed social media posts—oil paintings tend to be repetitive. Their subjects appear in the same poses and in the same style. The reason is that the oil painting was not so much an artistic expression as a proof of status. As the portable photo camera became a household item, taking pictures became an important ritual for all social strata. Just as oil paintings performed specific functions, so do photographs. In their study of photography, Pierre Bourdieu and his team show that what people picture and how they circulate the images simultaneously reflects and defines their social position. Like oil paintings, photographs are repetitive as they express a "system of schemes of perception, thought and appreciation common to a whole group" (Bourdieu et al. 1990, 6). Pictures are taken during important occasions, like weddings or graduations, when people congregate to reaffirm their commitment to those being celebrated (the newlyweds, the graduate) and to the institutions. Bourdieu and colleagues note that the intensity of photos fluctuates with intensity of family life; pictures are taken when ties are made or remade—think of babies, birthdays, and banquets.

Social media and mobile technologies have further increased the number of pictures and accelerated their diffusion. Visual records are now instant and ongoing. While its form and frequency have changed, photography continues to function as a means to register, affirm, and celebrate social bonds. Images and videos posted to Instagram, Facebook, TikTok, or Snapchat often register and celebrate social bonds using standardized poses and frames. However, we do see some shifts and variations. Although selfies constitute only a small proportion of social media posts (Caliandro and Graham 2020), this style of self-portraiture appears to be much more common now than it was in the past. This might explain why critics feel compelled to comment on the genre—it represents a shift in what Elias referred to as the "We–I balance," with the individual, instead of the group, being solemnized (Elias 1991a). Here, we begin to see how social media change not just the structure of our social relations, but also our sense of self and sensibilities.

Structural Pressures

Norbert Elias's work, in general, and his work on the absolutist court, in particular, presents a model of how to study simultaneous changes in relations and sensibilities. As such, it provides conceptual building blocks for our efforts to construct alternate mental models to understand social media. Initially written in the 1930s, *The Court Society* (1983) discusses the efforts by members of the French nobility to affirm and promote their status in the court of Louis XIV and his successors. Elias tries to understand the specific type of politics undergirding the exuberant displays of status of the French nobility of the late seventeenth century. Courtiers were engrossed in displays of status and engaged in intense predation. While status displays reflected formal status to some degree (a higher-ranked noble had more resources to invest in attire and could claim a more prominent seat at the banquet), aspiring elites were able to improve their position through diplomatic gossip and the staging of impressive performances of grandeur. For contemporary observers, Elias noted, it is tempting to project currently dominant values, like sobriety and thrift, on the French court and explain its exuberant displays as mere decadence.[3] Instead of merely denouncing exuberant status displays, Elias's goal is to uncover the structural pressures enticing people to act the way they did. Could we, analogously, identify the structural pressures exercised through social media? We think we can. There are important differences between platforms, but there are also structural pressures that operate across social media platforms and affect users to smaller or greater degrees. To fully grasp what social media are and do, we must grasp what is common to them before attending to the important variations within and between social media platforms.

First, social media extend and facilitate *mutual monitoring*. Through social media, people expose parts of their lives to others. Sometimes their audiences are unknown lurkers, sometimes they are close friends, but social media have mainly intensified what Mark Granovetter (1973) referred to as "weak ties." People are now more intensely and directly connected to distant others. While Granovetter, and many after him, considered weak ties as conduits for information (about jobs, for instance), such ties also are vehicles of social pressure and control. Elias argued that the extension and differentiation of interdependencies "requires and instills greater restraint in the individual, more exact control of his or her affects and conduct, it demands a stricter regulation of drives" (Elias 1994, 2:429). Social media are the carriers of these interdependencies because they bind people together—they bring people into view and in dependence of one another. Social media, in this reading, do not bring about disruption but represent one further step in bringing people closer together, for better or worse.

Second, social media *collapse the private–public division*. Social media enable and encourage users to exhibit public displays of their private selves. The public–private division, which scholars like Hannah Arendt (1958) and Michel Foucault (1979) identified as fundamental to bourgeois society and its public sphere, is blurred or absent. Private selves are not bracketed (as the public sphere paradigm would suggest), but they become instruments and stakes in the competition for status.[4]

Third, social media represent *stratified systems of rank*. While they compel users to exhibit individuality, at the same time they work to standardize individual expressions by imposing metrics, including numbers of friends, followers, or retweets. Such metrics rank users into an overarching hierarchy. Although clearly there are different subdomains or fields within social media, it is nevertheless possible to instantly rank social media users according to basic metrics and to assess their position within social networks. As several authors have noted, the competitive and evaluative logic of the once-popular website Hot or Not lives on in social media platforms (Losse 2012; Reagle 2015; Kotsko 2017). As users, we're all part of a system of judgment. The use of social media analytics to calculate a "social credit score," as has been proposed in China, is simply the consummation of this logic (Mau 2019). Instagram has started hiding certain metrics from users in the name of protecting well-being, but it has not "de-metrified" entirely (Rogers 2016).

Although they vary in intensity and nature between different platforms, these structural forces impinge on all social media users. Individuals may try to negotiate, deny, or disrupt these forces, but they cannot altogether escape them. Even deleting social media accounts and going offline provides no sure escape from symbolic hierarchies reflected and shaped by social media. Our "shadow profiles" exist not only in the databases of social media platforms, but also manifest in interpersonal offline encounters, where the fact of not being on Facebook frequently becomes a source not only of disbelief, but of distrust as well. Some employers reportedly pass over applicants that lack a Facebook profile, and columnists have advised women to pass on dating men without an active online presence. Increasingly, escaping social media is only possible by foregoing social relations. These structural forces elicit certain dispositions and sensibilities.

Dispositions

Let us first consider dispositions. When we look through the lens of relational sociology, our assumption is not that social media users are disposed to engage in debates premised on communicative rationality. Instead, we foreground their disposition toward *decorous status displays*. Social media users tend to post aspirational images that confirm or boost their status (Marwick 2013). They exhibit their talent and possessions through still life photographs, showcase their personas through selfies, celebrate their social ties with group pictures, and so on. What the sociologist Erving Goffman said of personal collections of photos is true also for social media posts:

> Thus it is in modern times—and as the modern contribution to ceremonial life—that whenever there is a wedding, an investiture, a birthday party, a graduation exercise, an extended voyage begun or terminated, a picnic, a shop opening, a vacation, or even a visit, snapshots may well be taken, developed, and the prints kept easy to hand. Something like self-worship can thus be accomplished. The individual is able to catch himself at a moment when—for him—he is in ideal surroundings, in association with socially desirable others, garbed in a self-enhancing way (which for white-collar men may mean the rough and manly wear of fishermen, hunters, wranglers, or machinists), poised for a promising take-off, terminating to an important engagement, and with a socially euphoric look on his face. A moment when what is visible about him attests to social matters about which he is proud. A moment, in short, when he is in social bloom, ready, therefore, to accept his appearance as a typification of himself. (Goffman 1979, 10)

A casual look at Facebook or Instagram suggests things have remained the same since the time of Goffman's writing, at least as far as the occasions and motivations are concerned. The snapshots "kept easy to hand" have now become scrollable grids of images, and they are shared in much higher numbers at much greater speed. The number of pictures taken each year has increased astronomically from an estimated one billion in 1930, to twenty-five billion in 1980, to 380 billion in 2012, to one trillion and more starting in 2014 (Mirzoeff 2015, 6). As devices to record, view, and share snapshots diffuse, people become ever more tightly integrated into a symbolic universe of status displays. As in the court society studied by Elias, acquiring a position requires not just attaining wealth or power, but clearly putting it in evidence in the field of vision. Although there are parallels with Thorstein Veblen's (1934) famous thesis on conspicuous consumption, Elias's analysis differs in that it shows how wider chains of social interdependence compel courtiers to play according to the rules of court rationality. Their predatory and flashy behavior is not the outgrowth of an "instinct," as it is in Veblen's *Theory of the Leisure Class*, nor is it properly understood as a manifestation of a culture of decadence. Elias helps to explain why some people—especially those at the very center of the symbolic universe—exhibit their status through impressive and forever changing attire and poses.

The logical correlate of displays of status is *predation*. Most social media users spend much more time viewing their feeds than actively posting. They show an interest in people they care about or news that matters to them. Such interest—regardless of its content or subject—tends to be normatively inflected and drawn to instances of transgression. Social media users do not only prey on signs of status decline but also, more positively, search for beauty, wit, or inspiration. But what are the meaningful markers of status? What are adequate displays? Finding this out requires monitoring both those with higher status as well as those who are more proximate. Superiors model what one aspires to, although their displays cannot simply be copied by those further down the pecking order without their appearing laughable. Socially more proximate individuals model displays that are adequate to one's own rank, but they, too, cannot simply be copied because to do so would mean not rising in the esteem of others but merely maintaining one's place. For that reason, those who aspire to achieve recognition—courtiers under Louis XIV or very active social media users today—are engaged in an arms race of stylistic distinction. Both audiences and stars are incessantly exchanging information on each other's character and status. A social media network functions as a gossip network in which people not only talk about each other but also volunteer information about themselves.

Status has been the key stake in these gossip networks throughout history, but its determinants have changed. There has been an ongoing process of social integration that has blurred categorical status differentials. Although social differences—along gender, racial, or class lines, for instance—continue to be crucial determinants of status differences (Ridgeway 2019; Piketty 2014), status has increasingly come to be seen as reflective of a uniquely individual character, not as derivative of group membership or one's location in social structures. Women, workers, the young, ethnic minorities, and sexual minorities have not achieved full equality, but they no longer have to defer to more established groups to the extent they used to (Wouters 2007). These shifts in the balance of power are indexed by a shift in language. The imperative to "check your privilege" reflects the ongoing challenges against inherited status superiority, just as the backlash against this language illustrates that this battle is far from over. Nevertheless, there has been a long-term trend away from categorical identities that are ascribed at birth and sustained through formal rituals toward personal identities sustained through informal rituals (Collins 2004). Consequently, status is experienced and pursued as a personal project: crafting self-images to demonstrate where we stand and to what we aspire has become a hallmark of contemporary culture and is the essence of social media.

To successfully navigate social media, users have to gain facility in what psychologists refer to as self-presentation and self-disclosure: they need to diplomatically present aspects of their identity and disclose intimate information (Valkenburg and Piotrowski 2017). When they succeed, users receive positive feedback and come to be recognized for who they want to be and what they want to show. Because users decide what and when they share, they can emphasize those parts of their lives that they feel most confident about. Recording moments can, by itself, heighten a sense of excitement and elatedness, and it appears that the vast majority of feedback on social media is positive (Diehl, Zauberman, and Barasch 2016). Not only upbeat posts receive likes and recognition; it has also been found that Instagram and Facebook users who report feeling depressed receive messages of support and consolation (Zhang 2017). Even in the absence of such positive feedback, the very act of building an online persona can be empowering and enchanting. Research among teenagers has found that managing an online profile often boosts self-esteem (Valkenburg and Piotrowski 2017, 229).

Notwithstanding these findings about the energizing effect social media can have, users are likely to experience friction between what they feel on the inside and what they show on the outside. What is true for holiday pictures featuring people in the thrall of the moment is also true for heartfelt disclosures of depression: they are not only put on display but also appraised (or ignored altogether, which is also a form of evaluation). Young people, in particular, are keenly alert to the ways their online personas and connections define their place in the social world (Milner 2016, 230–244; MacIsaac, Kelly, and Gray 2018). Members of the millennial generation are acutely aware of the dependence of their life-chances on a marketable brand. As Malcolm Harris (2017, 178) has observed, "opting out of social media is like hiding away in an attic. You just can't compete that way." Entire livelihoods, especially among freelancers, can come to depend on visibility labor (Abidin 2016b) and other forms of digital work (Gandini 2016; Scolere, Pruchniewska, and Duffy 2018).

Anxieties and Desires

Social media users thus face a dilemma. They can either selectively represent themselves to maximize recognition (and experience a contradiction between public display and private self), or they can represent themselves more fully (and risk ridicule and criticism). The flipside of ample opportunities for self-presentation and self-disclosure is that there is a tension between the carefully curated and crafted posts and everyday experience. This tension did not originate with social media, but it has been endemic to social life for as long as people have sustained extensive communication networks. It has also been central to sociological and social psychological theorizing. The imperative to manage impressions is, among other things, a central theme in Erving Goffman's celebrated work (Goffman 1959, 1986), and for Anthony Giddens (1991) the reflexive constitution of the self is the key challenge of modernity.[5] The idea that increasingly extensive and dense networks confront people with stringent and contradictory demands has been key to Elias's work. He considered it the sociologist's mission to elucidate the broader sets of relations that are at the root of individually experienced anxieties and desires. Seen in this light, social media do not represent a "revolution" in communication, but one further step in a long-term process of tightening interconnections that compel individuals to reflect on their own biographies and identities. Social media amplify and exemplify this predicament by requiring users to think about how they want to present themselves while confronting them with an endless stream of stylized self-images crafted by others.

Let us consider the story of David as an illustration of how social media are implicated in social relations and sensibilities. David, a journalist in his early fifties, told us that he "of course" has an Instagram account—"I have two teenage daughters." He took comfort in seeing pictures of his daughters partying at clubs, as he had learned to worry when they *didn't* post. As we went over the few posts in David's Instagram timeline, we encouraged him to say more about a picture featuring him and his eighteen-year-old daughter, Doreen, posing in the kitchen. It looked neat, like they really made an effort to stage the picture and choose the perfect filter.

But David insisted that he could not recount how the picture came about. "You have to understand, they take pictures all the time. Our days are filled with posing and looking at pictures." Although we did not learn much about the story of the kitchen photo, one thing became clear: that picture would never have made it into David's timeline without his daughter's explicit permission. "Every picture is screened!" He once posted a picture of his daughter on Facebook without asking her permission: "She was texting me within a minute. No, no! She actually *called* me. She called me! That hadn't happened in a *long* time. She thought that the picture showed a pimple. 'Take that picture down immediately!' " He did as he was asked.

Impression management took on a heightened significance after David and his wife got divorced. Following the divorce, David observed a change in his own social media use. "When I was an established family man, I posted pictures and shared happily." And now? "Now I'm ashamed." His own relations and those of his wife had become entangled on social media, so she would see any picture he posted, as would her friends and her relatives. As a result, he had stopped posting. His situation became even more delicate when he and his ex-wife started dating each other again. The divorce and the precarious make-up deeply disturbed his daughters. Arguments with them began to escalate rapidly, with insults aiming at complete denigration being hurled at David and his ex. His oldest daughter was furious with her parents who, she said, were "behaving like teenagers." She was embarrassed to the bone. "It hurts my eyes; I can't watch this." Arguments also turned physical. His daughter threw things at him and her mother, and she spat at them. They were having these fights all the time, they were taking pictures all the time, so the question arose: Do the pictures show the fights? Do the fights move onto social media? David hesitated, then answered, "Initially we feared that she might take the fight to Facebook. But she hasn't." So, none of these family feuds find their way to social media in any way? "No." The pictures remained happy, even glamorous.

What to make of these observations? None of them make sense from the perspective of the public sphere—we do not see anything like rational deliberation on issues of public interest. Another reading, along the lines of Christopher Lasch's diagnosis in *The Culture of Narcissism* (1979), would consider the protagonists in this story as self-involved in their attempts to craft a glorified version of their lives. Upon closer inspection, however, David and his daughters do not resemble Narcissus in any way (see also Senft and Baym 2015). Instead of falling in love with their own self-image, they see themselves through the eyes of others. Their self-monitoring served to keep their imperfections, of which they were keenly aware, from surfacing. Yet another take would be to consider social media users "shameless" (Senft 2020), but we actually see the opposite. Doreen scanned pictures for pimples and was deeply embarrassed by her parents; David felt ashamed and moved his conversations outside the public eye. The divergence between offline and online is striking. "Keep up appearances" is the precept by which all people in the story live. The interview also hinted at the reasons: there are many onlookers on social media, and they come from different circles. Considering that they wanted to avoid further shame and embarrassment, they had too much to lose by exposing their conflicts.

Beyond Media Effects

As media scholar Andreas Hepp (2010) notes, media and communication researchers have historically attempted to identify the "effect" or "influence" of different kinds of media (see also Williams 1975; Livingstone 2009; Marwick 2018). To give just one example of this kind of focus: when they attempt to establish whether Instagram use makes people happy or depressed, psychologists measure how people feel when they use the platform a lot or not at all and whether their moods improve or worsen after they used the app (e.g., Mackson, Brochu, and Schneider 2019). Such research can be valuable, but its foundational premise—that it is possible to isolate media effects—is becoming questionable as our social worlds are remade through social media. As argued in the introduction, TikTok, Instagram, Facebook, Twitter, and other platforms are not simply *added* to already existing social relations and arrangements but *change* them. As part of this transformation, social media have become *ecological* (Postman 2010). This should change how we assess and research social media. It means that the difference they make is no longer linear. Instead, they effect a broad qualitative shift that is not confined to any particular area, but that has reverberations throughout the social environment.

Let us mention one example to illustrate this point. At the time we met her, Sophie was an attractive twenty-seven-year-old philosophy graduate and fervent Instagram user. She had just 322 followers when we spoke to her, but she was gaining followers swiftly. After using Instagram casually for a couple of years, Sophie had decided she was going to get more involved during a study-abroad year on the island of Bali in Indonesia. She had observed influencers taking pictures during their holidays and figured out how to create picture-perfect images. During the interview, we noticed it was working. Her most recent story was receiving a steady stream of likes and comments that were a constant source of interruptions. Sophie was visibly pleased.

Now, were we to use standard psychological measures to assess whether Instagram makes Sophie happy or depressed, we would find that the effect is positive: she got a kick out of Instagram. But what was happening could not be captured by standard psychological scales. She was not simply "using" the app; she herself changed as she interacted with it. It is interesting that Sophie, like many others among our research participants, compared her Instagram use to a drug habit. The metaphor captures just how elated and enthralled she felt when she used Instagram, but also that she was under its spell. She speculated that what makes Instagram so important to her could be that she had received little validation in her romantic relationships or business adventures. Instagram gave her instant gratification, but she was fully aware that she not only instrumentalized the platform but that it also instrumentalized her. As someone who read both Marxist and neuroscience literature, she was acutely aware of how Instagram's programmers attempted to shape her dispositions and behavior. As Instagram became central to her life, she noticed that she looked at the world, herself, and her relations differently. She saw people through what they post on Instagram, while people who were not on Instagram disappeared from her view. This example shows that a research strategy that compares moments of social media use with moments of non-use, that tries to isolate "media effects," or that counterposes users to non-users, fails to capture something foundational: broad qualitative changes in the structure of social relations and selfhood.

Cities and Social Media

If we study social media as an integral part of everyday life and social formations, we must take an ecological perspective. We need to conceive of online interactions not as a realm apart, but as coextensive with the work we engage in throughout our everyday lives of presenting ourselves to others and interacting with them. Our online profiles now extend and supplement offline identities and relations. This also means starting our investigations at the interface of online and offline relations rather than privileging either realm.

The growing interdisciplinary scholarship on cities and digital platforms suggests different avenues to understand this interface. One influential strand, revolving around the notion of "platform urbanism," takes a decidedly critical perspective. Its proponents are particularly interested in the workings of a capitalism "centred upon extracting and using a particular kind of raw material: data"

(Srnicek 2017, 39). In platform urbanism, urban infrastructures turn into an annex of this mode of accumulation, serving to extract profit from users and cities (Rodgers and Moore 2018; Sadowski 2020). Researchers have chiefly explored the maneuvers of players in the "sharing economy," such as Airbnb and Uber, to undercut regulation in labor and housing markets (van Doorn 2017, 2020; Wachsmuth and Weisler 2018).

Other scholars emphasize variability and ambiguities of the digital city rather than an overriding, global logic of profit. They argue that digital technologies are not deterministic, that they allow for creative reinterpretation and reappropriation (Barns 2019; Degen and Rose 2022; Leszczynski 2020; Rose et al. 2021). Seen in this light, places acquire new layers of meaning as they are increasingly represented on digital platforms and experienced through digital media (Halegoua 2020; Krajina and Stevenson 2020; Rose 2022).

Instead of prioritizing systemic logics or local variability, we are interested in their *interplay*. We seek to understand the interface between social media and the city by examining how social media posts reflect and, in turn, shape practices, relations, and inequalities (Graham, Zook, and Boulton 2013; Shelton, Poorthuis, and Zook 2015). This requires us to pay attention to both the social *construction* and the social *production* of urban space; that is, how we give meaning to urban experience and how the city materializes (Low 2016; Beveridge and Koch 2023). Conceiving both cities and digital platforms as sites of socialization *and* as stages for status display, we set out to understand the social formations and hierarchies that emerge at the interface of digital platforms and cities.

Let us give an example from Javastraat, a shopping street in Amsterdam's Oost borough about which we will have more to say in Chapter 6. There we found Two Rivers Deli, a grocery store that, a few years ago, reinvented itself as a delicatessen store and take-out restaurant, selling fresh falafel and delectable North African and Middle Eastern specialties. Previously, the store catered mostly to working-class immigrants, but now its clientele consisted predominantly of white gentrifiers. Many immigrant-run shops on Javastraat feared they would have to close as a result of rent increases and the displacement of immigrants from the neighborhood; however, Two Rivers was flourishing. We cannot blame social media for these transformations, but they do figure into them. Aisha Tahiri, the aforementioned activist and entrepreneur helping immigrant enterprises, advised Two Rivers on how to change their product line and appearance to appeal to gentrifiers in the neighborhood. As part of the makeover, the store set up an Instagram account. Aisha noticed that newly arrived gentrifiers often tagged the store. "They want street credibility, it's a cool thing." Aisha described the new look as "Insta-proof," testifying to the extent to which the aesthetic sensibilities of a particular group of city dwellers are associated with the platform. Our point here is not that Instagram was responsible for the transformation of the store, but rather that it played a role in how changes occur and how we appraise them. Attempting to pinpoint the unique contribution that Instagram made is pointless exactly because it is part of broader transformations, including the gentrification of Amsterdam, the rise of new aesthetic registers, and changing consumption preferences.

The examples of the transformations in Sophie's life and in the streetscape of the Javastraat illustrate the need for a shift away from media-centric accounts (see Morley 2009; Hepp 2010; Couldry 2012). We need to make a paradoxical move: if we want to understand social media, we must direct our focus beyond them. We must situate media use in social and geographic environments to discover how they are implicated in the changing structure of social relations and shifting sensibilities and senses of self. For us, this means taking a macroscopic perspective to examine broad patterns of uneven visibility, and it also means studying up-close how people conform with, negotiate, and resist their positions within emergent hierarchies.

Social Media and Social Change

Social media are frequently imagined as vectors of transformation and disruption, concealing the continuities and conservative schemas that are reproduced by these platforms. In contrast to commentators who view social media as game-changing, disruptive, or revolutionary, our argument so far implies that they tend to reproduce and stabilize existing norms and hierarchies. The extension and densification of networks facilitated through social media generate social pressures to conform. Social media make it easier to find out what your position in the social order is and how you are supposed to behave. Social media also make it easier to spot and shame people who stand out (O'Neil 2022).

Occasionally, we get a glimpse of these pressures when prominent users reveal what goes on behind the façade that is their timelines. Essena O'Neill is a comparatively well-known and radical example.[6] After collecting over half a million followers on Instagram and earning a sizable income through product placements, the young Australian woman snapped out of it. She wrote that "social media is not real life," changed the captions of her posts to reveal the dreaded work that went into composing her seductive posts, and recorded a video message in which she broke down in tears as she talked about getting caught up in a world of deceit. The video went viral and made headlines around the world. Although O'Neill initially received praise, the backlash was intense. After she set up a campaign to crowdfund a book project, O'Neill's critics, including former friends, accused her of self-promotion. Her tearful epiphany, they suggested, was just an elaborate hoax. O'Neill lamented how social media induce people into putting on a show, but she found herself accused of fabricating a new online persona. She unwittingly illustrated the paradox that revealing the treachery of social media is itself considered treacherous—it is logically impossible to really believe someone on social media who tells you to distrust everything on social media. Faithfully adhering to the norms by trying to look your best and rejoicing in the attention can, ironically, look and feel more "real" than having a nervous breakdown and crying your heart out.[7] When she broke down and admitted she had been living a lie, O'Neill was considered, in her own words, "a genius manipulator" and a "brilliant actor." As long as she had been a "brilliant actor," she had not been called out as one. The accusations and death threats directed at O'Neill suggest that she was considered a traitor and a hypocrite. Playing along is not merely self-serving but is a tribute to the status hierarchy in which so much has been invested. Speaking out devalues and destroys the symbolic universe that has been created with the collective labors of countless users producing pleasing images and spotless streams.

The example of O'Neill illustrates just how difficult it is to upset social hierarchies through social media. The affirmation of social order is the rule, not the exception. Because we stress that social media users predominantly showcase that they conform to, or exceed, expectations, how do we account for the numerous debates raging on social media? Does our framework apply here, too? We argue that it can. In our reading, discursive contention does not signal communicative exchange so much as the embodied politics of status displays. Elias opposed the view of humans as *homo clausus*, in which the body is just a vessel for the true self. If we follow Elias and more recent scholarship insisting on cognition as an embodied process, what we call "a discussion" is often a series of position-takings meant to express identity and commitment rather than an exchange of arguments. Our political beliefs are not simply ideas that we hold in our heads, but ingrained dispositions (Bourdieu 2000).

Such a perspective is especially important when we want to appreciate why people can get so worked up about discussions: the opinions expressed and exchanged in such discussions are but the surface expression of deeply held beliefs rooted in an embodied ethos. This is true for O'Neill's former friends who accused her of hypocrisy, but it is also true for the pundits who spend their days defending their views and attacking others. What is at stake in these struggles is not simply an item on the agenda, but the legitimacy and value of an embodied way of seeing. This helps account for why people so rarely change their views (Kolbert 2017). Although the terrain and modalities of explicitly political struggles are peculiar, their logic is isomorphic to how fashionistas or foodies showcase their styles and tastes. Just as Bourdieu argued that we need "to abolish the sacred frontier which makes legitimate culture a separate universe" (Bourdieu 1984, 6), we suggest that we should not separate out (and thereby consecrate) public debate as a distinct sphere of activity. Bourdieu's work serves as a warning against an opportunistic eclecticism that would view exchanges on Twitter as "political discussion" while considering the sharing of pictures on Instagram as an altogether different type of activity centering on cultural expression. This is where we follow Bourdieu: we consider *all* social media expressions as status displays, regardless of their specific content. Just as an unending series of appealing scenes and bodies in Instagram feeds does not indicate the absence of politics, heated exchanges on Twitter do not signal the absence of status politics.

This is not to say that social media can *never* perform a role in fostering critique or progressive change, but they only do so under specific circumstances, and in specific ways. While accounts by Castells, Benkler, and others suggest that transformations of the media landscape are structurally conducive for dissent, we make an opposite argument by arguing that the new media landscape (like the old media landscape) is structurally closed but contingently open. If activists want to use social media, they must actively subvert its logic. Because dissent and criticism go against the grain, such subversion is a painstaking endeavor and challenging to sustain. Constant predation implies that social media users who speak out against the status quo are likely to face pushback, both in the short term, where they may face bullying and abuse, and in the long term, when digital traces of past activism come back to haunt them in job interviews. If activists are to use social media as a platform for expressing dissent, they must actively carve out a space and create an environment where different norms and pressures apply. Formidable pressures for conformity are perhaps nowhere more visible than in the obstacles, backlash, and repression faced by those seeking to subvert hegemonic norms on social media.

A New Model

Thinking about social media—what they are and what they do to us—is crucial at this juncture, when Silicon Valley's shiny promises are gradually being questioned. But there are old mental models that too often circumscribe how we think about the internet. This chapter has sketched a way forward, proposing that we break with inherited mental models by adopting an alternate prism. Understanding online interaction in terms of the public sphere amounts to a category mistake. By applying the wrong category, we fail to see and take seriously many of the social and cultural processes actually taking place in digital spaces. If, instead, we view social media as stages for status displays, they come into sharp focus. More than that, without a more encompassing perspective like the one proposed above, the new needs that social media platforms fulfill remain entirely elusive. When we view social media platforms as deficient public spheres, we cannot explain why people keep using social media despite the widespread belief that doing so is unhealthy, unproductive, and possibly even detrimental to democracy.

In this chapter we suggested that there are specific structural pressures which do not determine people's actions, but nonetheless shape the formation of sensibilities and habits. These include the observance of decorum and etiquette, predation, and the alignment of one's character with one's outward persona. Many of the processes we bring into focus here would either elude or irritate public sphere scholars.[8] The focus on appearance and gossip appears as a mere distraction when we consider social media as constitutive of a public sphere facilitating the exchange of information and opinions. But appearances and gossip appear in a different light when viewed through our lens: they are the lifeblood of status politics. Relational sociology and the broader framework developed in this chapter direct our inquiries as we seek to understand relations formed through Instagram, its ecology, and the desires and anxieties of its users.

When we argue for moving beyond the public sphere prism, we do not mean that we want to abandon critique. For instance, when we argue in Chapter 5 that social media produce not "fragmentation" but "integration," we do not mean a benign process where people with different preferences and interests come together in harmony. We view social media as stages for the expression of status that are characterized by mutual monitoring, the collapse of private–public distinction, and, most importantly, stratified systems of rank. What is essential to social media is not that people post updates and archive images, but that these contributions are appraised by proximate and distant others. Through close study of Instagram in Amsterdam, we hope to bring to the fore how social media's status politics change place, people, and relations.

3
Selves and Others

Sophie started her Instagram account during a year-long stay in Indonesia. She didn't feel like maintaining a travel blog, so she decided to use Instagram to document her experiences. At first, she planned to just post pictures on a private account that only her friends and relatives could access. Soon after she arrived, she decided that she might as well use the platform as a dating app, so she switched her account to public. Sophie quickly discovered that she couldn't just casually post the occasional picture, as she had originally intended. She encountered influencers in bars and on the beach—and on Instagram, of course—and noticed that she began imitating them. "I began making the typical Bali life influencer posts. I found it funny because there are so many influencers who take it so seriously. So I tried to be ironic." Sophie told us she did not know when exactly it happened, but she knew she soon crossed the fine line between irony and emulation.

When we met her, she had just posted a picture in an off-white outfit that she described as "not fashion-fashion, but influencer fashion." As we talked, hearts whirled across her screen. She remarked that "a horny twenty-two-year-old" had just commented. It wasn't clear if she felt flattered or insulted—probably a bit of both. By the time of the interview, two years after her stay on Bali, Sophie had, in her own words, "created a persona" on Instagram. Her bio read "Bohemian Beach Babe" and "Amsterdamse zweefteef," which roughly translates as "flighty Amsterdammer bitch"—a label she embraced after someone hurled it at her as an insult.

Sophie's story introduces three themes we will elaborate in this chapter. All Instagram users, like Sophie, have the opportunity

On Display. John D. Boy and Justus Uitermark, Oxford University Press. © Oxford University Press 2024.
DOI: 10.1093/oso/9780197629437.003.0003

to shape their self-presentation. This is often an emancipatory and joyful experience, as users creatively and playfully craft their profiles. An Instagram profile isn't simply a reflection of the self, but a work of aspirational labor that allows users to present themselves as they want to be. Instagram doesn't solve the problem of economic precarity or social insecurity, but it helps people to cope with such conditions as their profiles become the interface through which they pursue relationships and business opportunities.

However, and this is the second theme, such purposeful constitution of the self occurs within a stratified system of rank where visuals dominate and where competition is endemic. Just as the use value and exchange value of commodities exist in tension, so do the expressive and communicative aspects of social media posts: they are always more or less genuine expressions of the self, but they are also always more or less strategically crafted status displays (see Fiers 2020). In such a stratified system of rank it is not only difficult to be ironic, as Sophie discovered, but also to express grief or voice a political opinion. Viewers, as well as creators, of posts cannot avoid asking whether they are authentic expressions or strategically contrived, even if they acknowledge that the two are inseparable. Instagram thus becomes a stage where a conundrum of neoliberal society plays out: we must compete, but we also must stay true to ourselves.

A third theme we explore in this chapter is the difference between viewing and posting. While people generally post when they are at their most confident, aspirational, and energetic, they tend to view posts when they are distracted, bored, or feeling down. These divergent emotional states combine with the uneven networked nature of Instagram to produce a specific type of experience that is well-known to the average user. Scrolling on Instagram, it feels like almost everybody else is more successful, happier, and prettier. We show that Instagram users find different ways of coping with this predicament, but they can't fully escape it without leaving the platform.

As explained in more detail in the Appendix, the sample used in this chapter comprises twenty-one interviews with frequent users. The interviewees were aged nineteen to forty-three; five were male, the rest female. Most of our interviewees worked in creative professions, such as event organizing, music, fashion, or branding, but they also include a flight attendant, a project assistant, and a sound technician. Three interviewees were students, and two were out of work because of the COVID-19 pandemic. Four interviewees were Dutch with an ethnic minority background, while the others were native-born or internationals. All interviewees resided in Amsterdam at the time of the interview.

We feel it is expedient to study frequent and well-connected users, because they give us a good sense of what happens when Instagram becomes an important part of your life. The sizeable body of work on influencers and micro-celebrities also helps to understand this, but there are differences between these professional Instagrammers and the intensive users in our sample. We teamed up with Marije Peute to speak to Instagram users of varying backgrounds. Some of our interviewees benefited economically from their presence on the platform, but none of them relied exclusively or primarily on Instagram for job opportunities. Crucially, the people we talked to did not uniformly seek to maximize their follower count or monetize their accounts. While they cared about their number of followers and appreciated the attention their posts received, they were also apprehensive about the drawbacks of the platform. Their relation to the platform is fundamentally ambiguous as they play by Instagram's rules but also question them.

Crafting the Self through Instagram

Interviewees often describe their Instagram feeds as deeply *personal.* They want their feeds to reflect who they are; it is the self that should be on display. Kia described the posts in her Instagram account as a "portfolio" that represents different aspects of her character and life. She started using Instagram when she founded a CrossFit gym to share images of exercises, but soon discovered she could use the platform to document other important moments in her life. When she created her own account, she filled it with pictures that were significant to her. Kia's Instagram reflected her in a particular state of mind. "It's just the things that I see that are beautiful. Yeah. Sometimes I'm feeling super sexy, sometimes I'm feeling super strong, sometimes I'm in the mood for cooking with my children—I'm just sharing those moments on Instagram." Her feed was selective, even performative. "It's nice to create your life in a certain way," Kia said, admitting that her difficult moments do not find a way to her timeline. The result is a "getaway, kind of surreal world, a dream world," but it was still also quintessentially *her*: "it's personal." The images *should* be authentic, but they *are* almost always positive. This is less the result of careful calculation and deliberate curation than of an emotional dynamic. Kia would *want* there to be more vulnerability on the platform, but she *feels* like posting when she's at her most confident and ambitious.

This is not to say that there is no vulnerability or negativity in self-disclosure on Instagram. Of course there is (see Andalibi, Ozturk, and Forte 2015, 2017). It is just far more challenging to produce such posts (see Berryman and Kavka 2018). Daria, for instance, felt she had to commemorate her deceased friend Laura and devoted several posts and Stories to her memory. She received many likes and supportive comments, so it's not that there was a lack of affirmation, but she constantly thought about how people could interpret her messages and worried that people might question her integrity. Just as importantly, she questioned herself, concerned as she was for the posts to be genuine expressions of her grief, not covert calls for boosting her Instagram status. Questions like this rarely come up with boastful posts—certainly not to the same extent. Sharing peak moments comes naturally, which makes Instagram a platform for construing an idealized and stylized self.

Instagram doesn't only serve to document what people *are*, but shapes what they *become*. After finalizing her bachelor's degree in anthropology, Daria was taking on a number of short-term and part-time jobs. What she really wanted, though, was to become an illustrator. At that point, her account, under the artist name of Kopfkino, had only three hundred followers, mostly friends and family, but she felt that the platform was ideal for acting on her aspirations, so she alternated between posting selfies and illustrations. By developing her Instagram profile, her sense of self changed (Peute and Rus 2021)—a change that was reaffirmed after she landed a few gigs and got positive reactions from her small but intimate following. At some point she dared to take the step to make the change official:

> I still remember writing in my Instagram bio for the first time that I'm an illustrator. I wasn't officially an illustrator since I hadn't received any formal education, but I thought "I'm just going to do this." And then I suddenly started receiving messages from people who *actually thought* I was an illustrator. For a long time, a very long time, I felt that I was *claiming* to be an illustrator when I'm really not. But then I often looked at my Instagram and felt, "Well, it *looks* like I am. Yes, I am!" It was an affirmation that it was for real. It looked very neat, the Instagram page, because I very carefully selected the images I put there.

The affirmation wasn't just online. At parties and events, people started coming up to her to ask if she was indeed Kopfkino the illustrator. Her reputation as an illustrator was established well before she felt like one, and long before her illustrations earned her an income. While friends and acquaintances were complimenting her on her career, she was still doing odd jobs to make ends meet and agreed to bottom rates. But over time, her sense of self and professional success tracked her reputation. She started to get more jobs and she began to set higher prices. When we spoke to her, Daria had

Figure 3.1 Daria presents her new tattoos—her own illustrations commemorating a deceased friend—and comes out as an aspiring illustrator to her Instagram followers. Reproduced with permission.

tattoos of her own illustrations on both arms, and she wore a golden necklace engraved with her moniker (see Figure 3.1 and Figure 3.2). She had become the person she prefigured on Instagram.

As people document the high points of their lives on Instagram and turn the platform into a compendium of their qualities, views of the world, and social relationships, it becomes an anchor in their turbulent lives. While social media platforms are notoriously volatile (Bucher 2018, ch. 4; Bucher 2021), to our interviewees their Instagram feeds are a beacon, reminding them of who they are

Figure 3.2 Daria's necklace advertises her work as an illustrator. Reproduced with permission.

and what they aspire to become. Relationships in work and romance may come and go, but Instagram accounts stay. For creative professionals and artists, an appealing Instagram account with a high follower count provides an opening to potential clients or customers, reducing their dependence on gatekeepers, partners, or patrons. When a romantic relationship breaks down, Instagram is a pool of potential partners. In moments of stress or anxiety, the carefully curated feed is a source of comfort and confidence. The Instagram account is something to hide behind, hold on to, and live up to. In Giddensian terms, our interviewees engage in the reflexive constitution of the self against the backdrop of ontological insecurity (Giddens 1991). You might not have control over your life, but you can craft the interface through which you engage with others. But while crafting a coherent and pleasing profile can be uplifting and empowering (see Valkenburg and Piotrowski 2017, ch. 2), there is also a darker side to it.

Because there is so much that is *not* on display, interviewees experience a sense of alienation from the online persona that represents them, especially when they're feeling down, angry, or vulnerable. None of these states or emotions easily finds its way into Instagram Stories, let alone Instagram posts. At times when the need is greatest to build oneself up, making the investment into one's ego and one's relations is particularly arduous. Kia would want to "be more honest" and share moments of vulnerability, believing that those moments, too, define her, but she had not yet found a way. Sara posted with great frequency and was, by her own admission, always on her phone, and yet she felt estranged from her feed. "*Everything* I put on Instagram is tongue-in-cheek, because I know *exactly* how I profile myself. I'm constantly feeding. It's ridiculous, but the marketing narrative is always there." Samantha felt uncomfortable about her timeline representing her glamorous and confident side. She included a couple of pictures of her taking her grandmother for a walk, but they caused dissonance with her usual posts, rather than balancing them out. All these examples suggest that users have some discretion in how they use the platform, but also that they need to reckon with Instagram's vernacular and norms. Generally, they are formative of neoliberal subjectivity: timelines showcase consumption, success, and aspiration, while hiding stress, anxiety, and sorrow.

It is not that our interviewees want to hide these gloomier sides of their lives. Although a couple of (male) interviewees told us that they had no interest in expressing or seeing vulnerability, most of our (female) interviewees valued vulnerability and felt that it should be put on display. But it is challenging to do so. Daria's struggle to create space for mourning after her friend, Laura, died in a car crash, is illustrative. For one month after the accident, Daria found social media completely unimportant and didn't post at all. As someone who was very self-conscious, she found it taxing to think of ways to mourn the loss that would strike the right chord and resonate on the platform. She did an Instagram Story to share her grief and announce a series of posts on Laura. Her story received many responses from people who felt the same and her posts, including the bereavement card she illustrated, received many likes. This example illustrates that there is no taboo on sharing moments of vulnerability, but it does not come as naturally as sharing moments of success—it is a struggle that most people forego most of the time. Receiving large numbers of likes or comments is not an unambiguous form of affirmation (see Marwick and Ellison 2012; Marwick 2013, 11) because it raises the painful question whether the sharing of grief of vulnerability was actually just a strategic ploy to win recognition.

With politics, as with sadness or vulnerability, interviewees fear that their statements come across as insincere and opportunistic. When we were conducting a round of interviews in 2020, there was a wave of protests, both on the streets and on social media, prompted by the police murder of George Floyd in Minneapolis and the resurgent Black Lives Matter movement. One of our interviewees unreservedly expressed her support for the movement. Marije participated in Blackout Tuesday, a protest action against racism that had users around the world posting a single black square to their account, and she further added Stories to provide additional background and context to this symbolic action. Some other interviewees, though, felt ambivalent. Mark, self-described as "pretty woke" and a Black Lives Matter supporter, told us he had "an aversion against showcasing online." He believed some of his friends were doing just that. "I find it difficult to see some people sharing Stories and pictures," he told us, "even though I know for a fact that they are not committed at all and didn't read the books they're quoting from." But others marauded their peers for *not* speaking out. Mark and his partner were called out by friends for failing to express support. Daria, too, felt that the atmosphere was "toxic," as loyalty was expected, even demanded.

Instagram's mirage of representations makes it impossible to tell whether posts in support of Black Lives Matter stemmed from genuine support of the movement, fear of the repercussions of staying silent, or status-seeking considerations. Add to that a pressure to conform, and this epistemological quandary turns into a moral one. While these experiences and dilemmas are typical for white progressives in social circles where support for Black Lives Matter became, for a short period at least, the norm, Trinity, a Black woman, vicariously yet viscerally experienced predation of a different, more aggressive kind. Some of her Black friends speaking out against racism suffered from extreme online insults and threats directed at them. The possibility that she might be targeted discouraged her from speaking up. She already suffered from what she called a "constant stream of negativity" and did not feel strong enough to risk exposing herself to further harassment by speaking out on this struggle. She resigned herself to reporting users and pages that committed the most atrocious attacks against her friends. Although they are positioned differently, Mark and Trinity are both part of a symbolic universe that stratifies users, subjecting them to appraisal and predation. We pick up on the question of what happens when politics becomes part of status competition and predation in the next chapter.

Although the specter of "virtue signaling" looms particularly large when political beliefs are at stake (see also Kay 2020), it indicates a broader dilemma. Instagram users are haunted by the question of whether their posts reflect who they really are or what others want to see. Our interviewees paid very close attention to how their posts were received, monitoring how many comments and likes they generated. Faces and bodies, especially beautiful faces and bodies, do well. Several interviewees discovered that it's important to operate in a niche and produce a specific genre of picture: Daria did colorful and cheerful posts; Boris centered his art work; Patrick's feed was dedicated to fashion. Occasionally, they learned the hard way that some posts don't work well. Through feedback and by looking at more influential figures, interviewees learn to see like Instagram, scanning their environment for pictures that fit the vernacular and crafting posts that they know will do well. While interviewees felt that their feeds *should* be personal and authentic, a reflection of who they were instead of what others wanted them to be, they molded their Instagram persona in response to feedback they received through likes and comments, resulting in a conflict between the moral imperative to keep it real and the social pressure to keep up appearances.

Looking

Whereas *posting* is generally done with a great deal of reflection, deliberation, and strategizing, this is not the case for *looking*. Boris was on his Instagram "all day" when hung over, and Kia found herself checking her Instagram when she was doing "really nothing." People often scroll through their feeds when they're waiting in line, riding public transport, in situations where they want some distraction (like draining conversations, meetings, restroom visits, or lectures), and when they're too exhausted and drained to do anything more productive or rewarding. Users go to Instagram to escape the versions of reality presented to them by news media or more contentious platforms like Twitter. Trinity, for instance, described how she organized her feed to get humorous content to compensate for the constant negativity she was confronted with. She started her day with Instagram's Stories loop; it plays one after another "just like Netflix," and she "simply swiped" if she didn't like what she saw.

There is a certain irony in the fact that the posts that are curated and crafted with such care and consideration typically only receive cursory attention. Where posting is associated with the emotional intensity of excitement and anguish, viewing is usually low-energy and unfocused. Although they appreciate the content of their timelines, users often feel bad about browsing Instagram. It's comparable to fast food: it tastes good when you're feeling down, but it doesn't lift you up. Daria is an extreme example. She felt she would be more at peace if she was able to live in the moment, but she only rarely managed to do so:

> I was just watching the lightning one night for an hour and half straight. And then I listened to a podcast by a friend who was reading from books. I only listened. I didn't check Instagram or anything else. And then I watched the lightning again, and I was so happy. I know we live in the now and that all that mindfulness stuff makes me happier. But I just can't do it.

Daria's self-diagnosis was that she craved over-stimulation. She felt it was a way to avoid mourning her friend's death, to push away the thoughts that otherwise crept up on her. Instagram is where she got her fix. "I often keep on scrolling even though I know it will make me feel miserable. When I scroll I don't feel anything, I'm like a zombie, I'm switching off. When I finally put my phone away I'm so exhausted. But still, my thoughts come back and wake me up. And then I weep until I fall asleep."

Anxiety in a Stratified Systems of Rank

Although browsing doesn't usually involve a lot of intense affect, this doesn't mean that what people take in as they scroll doesn't affect them. It does, even profoundly so. When you're scrolling through your timeline while on the toilet or nursing a hangover, it doesn't feel like you're engaging in a formative activity. You're just killing time. But over the course of our interviews, respondents often became aware just how much time they were spending on the app and how it was shaping their sense of self and their views on their social environment.

Mark was one of those reflexive interviewees. He knew the pervasive and pernicious impact of social media all too well. An aspiring actor, Mark felt it was a professional necessity to be present on Instagram. It was not a stage he was comfortable performing on, but he felt he must. When Mark was in theater school, some of his classmates had already established their reputation and performed in theaters or movies. Their successes were invariably showcased online and occasionally entered into Mark's everyday life. He recounted taking a walk with a classmate who had starred in a recently released movie when they were stopped by a group of girls wanting to take a picture with his classmate. The movie had not been a blockbuster, but thanks to his Instagram presence his friend nonetheless got to act and feel like a star—the very definition of what Marwick (2013) describes as "micro-celebrity." Mark recalled this specific moment not only because of how shocked he was when it happened—"it was surreal!"—but also because of how normal it has since become to see friends, colleagues, and acquaintances being celebrated and totemized. It *was* surreal, but now it is commonplace. As Mark struggled to establish himself as a performer, his experience on Instagram was one of constantly looking up, absorbing the successes of people with more followers, gigs, and friends. It got to him:

> I was wondering, "Why am I thinking about this person that I haven't met in two years?" And then I realized, "Oh, it's because I'm reading his Instagram Stories almost every day." These people I was thinking about, they were often people I was looking up to; people that I envied because of their career or because of they were they presented themselves. And then, when I put my phone down, these people were on my mind. They almost haunted me.

He recalled one particular person that haunted him. "I had an obsession with that guy. He was just, at least in my opinion, in every way more creative, capable, and attractive than I was." The confrontation was too much for Mark, so he decided to unfollow his scourge, banning him from his life and thoughts—until he met him again in a shop. "Bang! I was engulfed by stress and anxiety." For a moment, Mark recalled feeling paralyzed, but he had learned, through therapy sessions and self-help websites, to overcome this bout of anxiety. He pushed himself to have a chat and discovered that they could have a polite conversation. The myth was busted. Still, it was hard emotional work.

Mark's anxiety was often compounded by the fact that his boyfriend was one of the people doing better in life and on social media. As their social circles were interlinked, Mark's timeline was often filled with the people who spent time with his boyfriend. Although he didn't want to check in on his boyfriend, that's what he found himself doing when he looked at Stories where his boyfriend appeared alongside his friends. Experiencing those social occasions without being a part of them was alienating, in part because Mark felt he really didn't have a legitimate reason to complain, and then remained quiet about his feelings.

This sense of alienation didn't even go away when Mark participated in the performances to which he was usually a mere spectator. At the height of the COVID-19 pandemic, Mark and his boyfriend went into isolation abroad, on what he described as a "fairy-tale estate." They were accompanied by a group of high-school friends, many of whom were forced to spend their days in isolation. In these unusual circumstances, the group enjoyed an "Alice in Wonderland" type of experience during their retreat which, naturally, had to be broadcast. He recalled a day that was so hot that they all wanted a good soak. But before they had even pulled out the hose, the others had already gotten their phones out, ready to capture the moment and package it into slow-motion clips. The times he enjoyed the most during their retreat were moments with no phones around to look at or record, but those moments were rare—most of their time spent together was in anticipation of and in response to social media. Mark realized that they often did not just document what they happened to be doing, but they did things *in order to* document them—they construed reality so that it could be represented. Perhaps that was even true of their group as a whole. "To outsiders we must have looked like best friends, a real community," Mark reflected, "but I wondered what sort of connection we shared."

Mark might look like an extreme case, someone who is unusually self-conscious or anxious. That was, at any rate, what he himself believed, and his fears about his work and social relations prompted him to consult a psychologist and websites to learn cognitive behavioral therapy skills. Part of the reason he wanted to talk to us was that he felt it to be important to reflect on how he might change the impact social media has on his life for the better. When we spoke to him, he told us that he had come to terms with social media. In fact, he believed that social media is what you make of it, and he had gone some way toward learning to use Instagram playfully and creatively. He decided to talk to the person who was so intimidating to him, and found out that he wasn't nearly as impressive in real life as he loomed in Mark's imagination. After this experience, he tried putting his phone away and only looking at it together with his boyfriend. He concluded that he probably wouldn't have matched particularly well with the people on the retreat even if there had been no social media. An anxious person with a strong tendency toward social comparison—a group found to be at risk from suffering mental health issues due to social media use (de Vries et al. 2018)—can nonetheless cope with the pressures of Instagram and build up resilience in face of the constant onslaught of alluring images.

Unique as it is, there are aspects to Mark's story that point to larger structures beyond his control. Most fundamentally, social media permeate his world—whether or not he chooses so. That is true for budding performers, as well as students in middle and high school. It is common for young people to join Instagram long before they turn thirteen (the minimum age to have an account according to Instagram's Terms of Service), and status on the platform is strongly associated with status in offline social relations (MacIsaac, Kelly, and Gray 2018; Krogh 2023). Abstaining from Instagram means foregoing potentially important social opportunities. Instagram is an offer you can't refuse—at least not without considerable cost.

Like other users, Mark did not get to choose his position in the stratified system of rank that is Instagram. His position was about where most people are: connected to the center but not quite in it. It is a now classic sociological insight that our friends usually have more friends than we do (Feld 1991). This is called the "friendship paradox," and is a result of the unequal distribution of friendship ties within social groups. Because many things are distributed in a similarly unequal manner, sociologists have posited a "generalized friendship paradox." Our friends are not just, on average, more popular than we are, they are also happier, more interesting, positive, powerful, special, and important (Grund 2014; Bollen et al. 2017; Zhou, Jin, and Zafarani 2020). These patterns result from uneven network structures: happy, interesting, positive, and powerful people have more social ties than others. This discrepancy is further amplified on social media through highly uneven networks that are organized around key figures. Not only are your friends on Instagram more likely to *actually* be more successful, but they are also likely to *exaggerate* their success by construing an idealized and stylized self. And, on top of all that, they also tend to present themselves when they're at their peak, while you are likely to view their posts when you're down. For most users most of the time, browsing Instagram means looking up in the social hierarchy. One way in which they experience this hierarchy is through what we may term the "excitement paradox." Commentators have devised labels such as "toxic positivity" or the "good vibes only mentality" for this experience, noting that it can be psychologically draining to expose oneself to images that almost without fail carry a positive, happy valence. Sociologically, the excitement paradox may also bolster the differences between ranks by privileging certain selves and their capabilities to feel in appropriate ways (Ahmed

2010; Cottingham 2022). Feelings are not private affairs, but they can have a practical significance that goes far beyond an individual experience. Incidentally, we believe such inequalities also serve to explain how norms and behaviors can cascade so rapidly on Instagram. From pictures of latte art and bucket challenges to black squares and avocado toast, they trickle down the social hierarchy through emulation.

Just as Mark's experience of looking up isn't unique, neither is his sense profound of alienation and confusion. All our interviewees emphasized in one way or another that what they see on Instagram is staged and selected, but nevertheless these are the images through which they come to see others and estimate their position in the social hierarchy. The ideals they see on display are not dependable, but they are still ideals. This is the shaky ground on which the project of constructing a self plays out. Interestingly, although some scholars emphasize that reconciling such unattainable ideals with a desire for authenticity results in feelings of shame (e.g., King 2020), our interviewees did not dwell on such feelings. Coping with the fickle companion that is Instagram involves not just a single psychological mechanism, but a variety of ways of making do.

Conclusion

Social media use has been woven into the fabric of everyday life, resulting in major transformations of how we feel, view ourselves, and connect to others. While early on many commentators were hopeful about the new opportunities for horizontal communication, the tides have decisively turned. An outpouring of documentaries, reports by non-governmental organizations, and opinion pieces sound a warning klaxon against social media's corrosive impact on psychological health and social relations.

Some psychologists have blamed social media for a wide range of contemporary problems, as indicated by the full title of Jean

M. Twenge's (2017) widely discussed book, *iGen: Why Today's Super-Connected Kids Are Growing Up Less Rebellious, More Tolerant, Less Happy—and Completely Unprepared for Adulthood.* Recently, Twenge has been joined by psychologist Jonathan Haidt in ringing the alarm about the "collapse" of mental health caused by social media. And yet, the extensive and continually growing body of psychological research on how social media affect people's well-being and their relations to others has so far yielded surprisingly few robust results. In a large-scale panel study, researchers from the Oxford Internet Institute find that the "relations linking social media use and life satisfaction are . . . more nuanced than previously assumed. . . . Most effects are tiny—arguably trivial" (Orben, Dienlin, and Przybylski 2019, 10228). The effects are so small and the correlations so complex that statistical models often—in about half of the cases in the Oxford study—do not find any effects at all. Looking specifically at Instagram, Beyens et al. (2020) find that adolescents, on average, felt slightly better after viewing posts or stories. Active Instagram use, though, had neither positive nor negative effects on well-being. Other studies, too, find mixed effects: sometimes Instagram use lifts people up, sometimes it pulls them down (de Vries et al. 2018). Effects are not just mixed but are also ambiguous. The Dredge and Schreurs (2020, 901) review study, for instance, documents a wide range of paradoxical effects: social media use correlates with a sense of belonging *and* with perceived isolation, with social capital *and* with relational aggression. Chatzopoulou, Filieri, and Dogruyol (2020) find that male Instagram users feel more anxious and in competition, but *also* feel that their self-confidence and motivation increase as they look at posts by muscular peers.

What accounts for these unspectacular and confusing findings? How is it possible that no effects are registered even in users who spend multiple hours a day on Instagram? The reason is not that impacts are absent or trivial, but that they are variable and ambiguous. Sometimes Instagram use lifts people up, sometimes it pulls them down; sometimes Instagram helps foster rewarding and strong connections, sometimes it corrodes self-confidence. While most of the literature attempts to unravel the impact of social media through sophisticated statistical analyses of survey data, we used qualitative methods, focusing on the situations and circumstances shaping Instagram use rather than background characteristics. Using such a set of methods, we find that Instagram results in qualitative transformations by changing the ways people are composed and connected. Instagram is not something that is simply *added* to the social worlds of adolescents and others who use the platform; it recreates worlds. Social media do not independently cause an effect, but they become an interface through which relations between the self and other are reconfigured. In this web of interdependence, social media do not determine what happens, but neither are they passive. They shape the interactions that they facilitate in ways we outlined in Chapter 2. There we argued that social media are stratified systems of rank that dissolve the public–private divide and facilitate predation. Looking specifically at Instagram, it entices and compels users to put themselves on display using photography, video, and captions. What sorts of dependencies, dispositions, and relations develop through such an interface?

We suggested that people reflexively constitute their relations and compose their selves online. People are not able to overcome ontological insecurity in their professional lives, friendships, and romantic relations, but they *can* cope with it by interacting with others through an interface that allows them to shape their self-image. Instagram specifically—and social media profiles generally—offers an opportunity for continuity and control in a social and economic environment where precarity and volatility are the norm.

One reason the potential negative effects of social media use identified in the psychological literature (like low self-esteem, depression, or narcissism) are not very pronounced is that people develop different ways to mitigate or counterbalance them, ranging from simple measures, such as unfollowing people that make them envious, to more fundamentally reflecting on who they are and what they want from life. These reflexive strategies mean that there is no unilateral impact of Instagram on its users. Instead, they creatively and reflexively struggle, adapt, and play with Instagram's functionalities and, by implication, with their relations to others and themselves.

And yet, Instagram isn't infinitely malleable. It is, in essence, a stratified system of rank, crystallized in uneven network figurations, that is organized around the attainment of status. Although our interviewees wanted to express themselves in a genuine manner, it is inescapable that their displays were appraised in a competition for attention and recognition. Instagram pushes users to promote themselves and create a persona that is easily consumed. The logic of branding dictates that they send out signals that people can grasp and are likely to appreciate. Although the reflexive crafting of a relatable persona is a task our interviewees take on with creativity and conviction, the tension between the polished online image and the complex offline reality also results in stress, alienation, and anxiety as they wonder whether they're worth the esteem of others and capable of living up to expectations.

4
Curating Contention

"How did you get into feminism?" In the context of Instagram, this may well come over as a loaded question because of the widespread assumption that Instagram feminists don their identities as feminists in the same way that some Instagrammers put on a new outfit from Zara—and that they are just as likely to discard it again once it has earned them some likes.[1] That clearly wasn't the case for Yasmin, though. A twenty-five-year-old artist and content creator based in Amsterdam, she began her answer by telling us about her relationship with her mother. Her mother grew up in the 1970s and 1980s, exposed to women's studies and feminist thought. "That really informed her way of thinking," Yasmin observed. "I was raised by her, she was a single mom, so she had pretty much sole input of what values I was soaking up." Yasmin's mother didn't forbid her from watching television shows with the occasional misogynistic joke, but she made sure her daughter was sufficiently aware to recognize them as such.

When Yasmin picked up a dusty feminist pamphlet as an adolescent, she was primed to respond well to its message of sisterhood. Even though her mother never pushed it on her, she enthusiastically embraced a feminist identity on her own—until she started reading about global feminisms as an undergraduate. Whether it was Chandra Mohanty's (1984) blistering critique of the "colonial discourses" embedded in western feminist thought or another of the ground-breaking texts that forced a reckoning with some of feminism's blind spots, she didn't recall exactly. But she did remember feeling shaken. "This is not dovetailing neatly with my identity as a feminist. Because I'm also mixed-race, and I'm also

On Display. John D. Boy and Justus Uitermark, Oxford University Press. © Oxford University Press 2024.
DOI: 10.1093/oso/9780197629437.003.0004

reading this argument, and I'm feeling really like this is actually kinda true, feminism isn't really including brown women, and it's sort of applying these ideas about sexuality and identity to brown women's communities, which are colonized in the first place." Her relationship to feminism has been fractured ever since, although she never repudiated the label altogether. "Those limitations I was just describing, they haunt me a little bit. Even when you wrote me—'You hashtagged feminist art, and that's why I'm reaching out'—I almost felt a little bit guilty." Haunting, guilt, an uneasy fit? This does not sound like a vapid identity put on for likes.

The previous chapter showed that Instagram users construct their selves on the shaky ground of a mirage of representations, doing their best to avoid negative affects as they define their place in the world by posting, looking, and connecting with others through the platform. The experiences of several of our interviewees suggest that taking a sincere political stance under such conditions is challenging. In this chapter we turn to the example of Instagram feminists to investigate what kind of politics can take shape in such a context. Instagram is a crucial terrain for the definition of contemporary feminism (Banet-Weiser 2018). How do feminists express or suppress their convictions on the platform? What sort of struggles do they engage in, both with others and internally? And how do they reconcile their political beliefs with their aesthetic sensibilities?

To answer these questions, we teamed up with Laura Savolainen, who was first a research intern and then a thesis student working with us at the University of Amsterdam, and who interviewed twenty-five self-identified feminists who were also Instagram users. We reached out to individuals who, like Yasmin, simply used words or hashtags associated with feminisms in their bios or post captions. All of them looked at Instagram content daily, while active posting ranged from daily to monthly. Aged between eighteen and thirty-seven at the time of the interviews, they represented about a dozen nationalities, and most had attained an academic degree. Four interviewees identified as LGBTQ+, with two of them identifying as non-binary, and all others as female. While our interviewees were overwhelmingly European, five resided outside of Europe at the time of the interview, and some were migrants from outside Europe or, like Yasmin, had parents who were. They endorsed a variety of feminisms, and it was common for their politics to consist of a bricolage of slogans or concerns from the historical "waves," such as individual empowerment, sex positivity, or collective action. Most engaged with feminist issues, such as rape culture, body positivity, or equal pay, and a few took part in feminist organizing on the ground. Their follower counts ranged from three hundred to over seventy thousand. Although our sample of interviewees is not representative, it reflects "the diversity and shifting nature of various feminisms and the fluidity of their boundaries" (Prügl 2015, 615). Thirteen interviewees gave repeated, explicit, informed consent to reproduce their public Instagram posts, both in the article on which this chapter is based (Savolainen, Uitermark, and Boy 2022) and in this book. The Appendix provides additional details on how we recruited the interviewees for this chapter.

Being Political on Instagram

Yasmin told us that, despite her numerous misgivings, she still felt excited and empowered by contemporary feminism. This was part of what drew her to Instagram, where she sought out the kinds of perspectives she craved, even as she continued to find inspiration in texts associated with earlier waves of feminism. She appreciated not being beholden to editors or other cultural gatekeepers deciding what she should see, and she particularly enjoyed browsing hashtags related to feminist art and to fashion for curvy women of color.

As for her own posts, Yasmin told us that, at first, she didn't think too much about what she added to her array of squares—her posts mostly consisted of closeups of her paintings—but the more we talked about it, the more it became apparent to her and to us that she did think about it *a lot*. We spoke about things she wouldn't post. This included most images of herself, especially if they could be construed as sexual. The idea of her employer seeing them, or future employment prospects being spoiled because of them, cast a shadow and caused her to hold back from posting such images. Her usual confident self-assurance gave way to another set of doubts. "I think I struggle with this a lot in terms of my own identity," said Yasmin. "What am I afraid of, why am I afraid to allow this to circulate, why am I afraid to own it in my own way?" She described her inner struggle as a war, with the part of her that sees women taking control of their own image as an inherently radical act facing off with another side of her that abhors exhibitionism. Resolving this tension meant making strategic decisions and difficult trade-offs. As she curated her profile, Yasmin toned down some of what she wanted to put out there, while amplifying other things that helped her gain access to people. "I can barely remember a time when I wasn't performing, in some way, a version of myself on the internet," she reflected.

Like Yasmin, many contemporary feminists engage in what we call *filtering* (Savolainen, Uitermark, and Boy 2022). This has repercussions for the circulation of feminisms in the economy of visibility of which Instagram forms a central hub. In this chapter we map out some of the practices associated with filtering by considering our interviewees' accounts of how they use Instagram alongside their posts. This helps us to understand not only how they use Instagram; it also offers a view of what empowerment means for them and what political projects they pursue or foreclose in their daily lives with the platform.

What do we mean by filtering? In its general use, filtering means to "remove something that is not wanted" (Oxford Advanced Learner's Dictionary 2023). In image editing, filters either *transform image data* or *generate new data to achieve a visual effect*

(Manovich 2013). Emergent feminist visibilities are filtered in this dual sense. Their digital mediation not only leaves elements out; it refashions. Filtering practices result from the need to resolve internal "wars" like the one Yasmin told us about. The users we spoke to sought to reconcile several contradictory desires: displaying status versus "candid" sharing, self-branding versus fighting structural inequality, attaining recognition versus not wanting to come off as overly thirsty for attention. Sometimes filtering works in a "subtractive" manner: it requires users to hold back and downplay what they otherwise consider to be intrinsically part of their selves. In other cases, however, interviewees' feminist sensibilities seemed to thrive on Instagram. Rather than filtering something *out*, filtering worked to augment their feminisms. We call this form "enhancing" filtering. Most often, however, filtering comprises subtle ways of making do with the frustrations of Instagram, resulting in *minute deviations*. Through subtleties of curation and composition, users try to let alternate ways of seeing and being shine through, even as they make compromises to accommodate the norms of Instagram's visual idiom and its status-centered mode of interaction.

Filtering Out the Offensive

As we spoke about how they craft their profiles, many of our interviewees found that they try to avoid evoking negative responses. Perceived audience expectations act as a constraint, particularly for interviewees in smaller and more conservative cities who were aware of their local followers' suspicion toward all things feminist and left-wing. Lotte, twenty-three-years-old and living in a small town in the Netherlands, worried about the social cost of being known as a killjoy. "I've been a bit in trouble, because I've been quite an extreme leftist," she told us. "Now that I'm living here, I don't feel comfortable showing my feminism on social media.

I don't post as many political things as I would like to. When I was living in Amsterdam, it was different. I felt more encouraged."

Lotte was not alone in holding back. Most other interviewees, however, were at a stage in their lives where their social circles and most of their Instagram followers were pro-feminist, which made it easier for them to wear their politics on their sleeve. But even then, expressing dissenting views could result in social sanctions, as experienced first-hand by Ajda. A writer in her late twenties whose parents settled in Sweden as refugees, she told us that she lost feminist friends after starting a meme account satirizing white Instagram feminists failing to see their own privilege. She dropped the project after less than a week. Fearing for their reputations, our interviewees—often reluctantly—abstained from posting images or comments that could cause discomfort for those on the receiving end. Instagram is not the place to hash out the finer points of power structures in which some users themselves are implicated.

Our interviewees learned to see their Instagram profiles as a form of social or aesthetic capital, so they guarded against sullying them. This was especially a concern for those facing an uncertain professional future. Faced with precarious prospects, they began to see self-presentation as a means to boost their professional chances. Depending on how they hoped to make their livelihoods, this may even be a requirement (Duffy and Wissinger 2017; Poell, Nieborg, and Duffy 2021).

Several people we spoke to reported feeling friction between what the pursuit of job opportunities demanded and how they would like to present themselves. Sara, a plus-sized model, reflected on how she used self-branding to define her professional self. Garnishing her posts with hashtags such as #Bold, #NoWrongWayToBeAWoman, and #EffYourBeautyStandards, she made her feminism central to her brand. While Sara's promotion of feminism contributed to her profile, she was reminded that she should not take it too far. On the advice of her agent, who told her that "feminism-related stuff can scare people away," Sara decided "not to post anything that men could find aggressive or wouldn't like." While she found this a hard choice to make, she also didn't find it too limiting. She opted for "sweeter" posts that would be more relatable. Specifically, she pivoted from intersectional feminism to posting more about autism awareness, a topic she found people could feel educated about without having to feel judged. We can think of her posting this kind of content as a form of "relational labor" (Baym 2015) that allowed her to connect with her audience's needs and expectations.

Erika, a professional feminist activist based in New York, also relied on Instagram to promote her work. Her occupation granted her more leeway in expressing her political views than Sara's, but she still felt constraints. She aspired to express "a feminism that has a more structural and economic critique," but found Instagram ill-suited to such ends. "Instagram is so visual, you have to show yourself all the time. And it makes for a feminism, or an activism, that is so centered on your own body, and not your thoughts, always . . . . I do think it's difficult . . . because I find that what I want to say really fits badly with the platform." Coming to terms with the conventions of Instagram became another struggle requiring trade-offs.

Of course, it *is* technically possible to use Instagram in a way that's more akin to how Tumblr is used, to post not just images but longer texts as well. But our interviewees had learned that that is simply not done. They subscribed to the view that Instagram is reserved for photographic, person-centered, and aspirational content. In other words, they felt constrained, not only in terms of the content they could post, but in the form as well. Instagram is not the place to express anger, vulnerability, or frustration. As we already learned in the previous chapter, posts expressing vulnerability or negativity are far more challenging to produce than the standard fare.

The anxieties and emotions at the root of subtractive filtering vary, ranging from worries over being able to "make it" with a reputation for militancy, to concerns about posting jarring content that will be seen as out of place by one's followers or as unrelatable and aggressive by powerful men. Invariably, the practice of subtractive filtering means submitting to the power relations that provide the ground rules of interaction on Instagram. These forms of filtering are contrary to the "zero fucks given" attitude behind popular slogans circulating on Instagram. Emotions, too, are subject to subtractive filtering, and of the gamut of emotions that motivate social movements—from outrage or frustration to hope and desire—few find their way onto the platform. Considering both feminist literature emphasizing the need for articulating critiques that are disturbing or uncomfortable (Ahmed 2017) and our interviewees' own insistence that it should be okay to show one's "true self," it is remarkable that negative emotions and vulnerable states are filtered out almost completely.

Feminism Enhanced

In contrast to these anxieties about holding back, some interviewees felt no such misgivings and, in fact, found the need to be relentlessly upbeat in alignment with their understanding of feminism. Explained a young art student named Jie, "Because feminism is all about paying attention to women, if you position yourself like, 'I'm not good enough,' you can't really show that to other people."

Some feminist practices and sensibilities thus thrive on Instagram. Case in point: Ida, a twenty-nine-year-old Danish student who saw herself as part of a fourth wave of feminism. She told us that she embraced labels like "whore" that were flung at her for her sexually suggestive Instagram profile. Her feminist awakening took place after she noticed how people discounted her academic expertise because she was into twerking, a dance characterized by thrusting one's hips while squatting. She became passionate about breaking norms and double standards related to gender and sexuality. She carved out a niche for herself as a feminist twerk-dancer-slash-activist. "I always say—it's kind of a joke—'I lure them in with my butt, grab them, and put feminism in their head.'" In effect, she wielded a weaponized femininity. She understood markers of normative femininity as resources to be mobilized in her battle against patriarchy.

Instagram turns out to be compatible with a branded, hyperconfident, and corporeal mode of activism like Ida's. She never tones it down. "My ass is a really big part of my brand," she told us. If people have a problem with her sexual assertiveness, that's fine. She takes it as a sign that she's transgressing boundaries. She makes the most out of Instagram's *affordances*—the platform's "possibilities for action" (Norman 1988, ch. 4)—and puts them to use for her own ends. This means gaining facility in the platform's visual features and figuring out what kinds of images and videos provoke the strongest reaction in her audience. Over time, she has modified her self-presentation for maximum engagement in the form of comments and likes. Through such continuous feedback, Ida not only gained algorithmic visibility and followers; her online persona gradually morphed into a lavish caricature. She has harnessed metrics and visibility for strategic purposes, and the results speak for themselves. Weaponized femininity has given her a platform. One time, she called out a popular dating site that asked its users to provide their skin color. "The website actually responded, 'We're so sorry, we're going to change it.' And I was like, it was a little bit of power there!"

Dutch activist Annette had a similar trajectory. She started posting YouTube videos as a young teenager and found that her sex-positive message strongly resonated. When we spoke to her, the twenty-three-year-old had become a micro-celebrity. By posting about her experiences as a bisexual woman and giving practical advice on topics such as oral sex, she hoped to educate girls and young women with less sexual experience. Her social media presence gave her a platform to advocate against slut-shaming and to insist that women are entitled to sexual freedom and pleasure.

Ida and Annette initially used Instagram to share funny moments with a small group of friends, but as they gained followers and branched out, they each started giving more thought to their image. Feeling a desire to "build an audience" or to be "discovered" by other Instagram users, their careers advanced from artless and spontaneous sharing to careful curation and self-promotion. Seeing the responses to their own posts and what others saw fit to post, they became increasingly aware of what works on the platform. They learned, for instance, that selfies work better than group photos or landscapes. This learning process, as well as changing technology such as improved smartphone camera lenses (let alone image editing apps like Facetune), gave rise to new aesthetic norms, expectations, and standards. Feminist expressions on Instagram are subject to such emergent norms as well.

Eve, an Amsterdam-based graduate student, helped us understand another implication of this learning process. "I wouldn't say feminism really stopped me from posting things—I actually posted *more*. Empowerment has a lot to do with it. It's important for me to have the courage to post some things—like more revealing photos—and not be afraid of what people will say. It really feels good to love myself and share it." Three things came together in Eve's story. First, she felt a push toward greater visibility because she was using Instagram; second, she had an ambition to build her profile as a true representation of herself; and third, her feminism helped reduce any inhibitions she may have felt about putting herself on display. As a result, her sense of feminist empowerment became entwined with aspirational self-presentation.

Eve wasn't the only one whose empowerment was an individual feat of display. Josefien equated feminist self-presentation with self-confident nonchalance. The twenty-two-year-old aspiring performer told us, "I feel like, as a woman, you can do whatever you want. If I wanna kiss a girl, or a friend of mine . . . or smoke a cigarette, and that's a cool picture, I can put it online." Rebecca opted to showcase her thriving career in the fashion industry (see Figure 4.1): "I think part of feminism is also taking up the space you

Figure 4.1 Rebecca's thriving career. Reproduced with permission.

deserve, claiming the credits you deserve and show[ing] the stuff that you're proud of."

In all these cases, feminist expression on Instagram is (not exclusively, but primarily) a matter of taking credit for personal accomplishments, be they aesthetic, social, or professional. As the writer Jia Tolentino has noted, today it is often "seen as unfeminist to criticize anything that a woman chooses to make herself more successful—even in situations . . . in which women's choices are constrained and dictated both by social expectations and by the arbitrary dividends of beauty work" (Tolentino 2019, 80). Beauty work indeed reaps dividends in the form of likes and comments. As our interviewees repeatedly told us, selfies receive the highest levels of engagement, and "sexy selfies" do particularly well. Many interviewees agreed that posed photographs can be an expression of a woman's self, sexuality, and empowerment.

Ajda, the writer and daughter of refugees, experienced social expectations even more urgently. She told us that, "[a]s a woman of color, I've felt the need to take myself seriously and present my accomplishments [on Instagram] in a way that's going to enhance the image of me as successful and good at what I do." Instagram was important to her because she had few other opportunities to brandish her professional accomplishments or "sharpen her elbows." Having recently ended a relationship with a controlling partner, Ajda also struggled with the ambiguity of "sexy selfies" and other ostensibly empowering images, noting that "a person who sees this photo doesn't see the struggle behind it." Her position as a woman of color gave her a different view of her own image. "My body is white-passing, I'm skinny, I have big breasts, I'm normatively pretty." She came to notice that the attention such images drew—that rewarded her for her desirability first and foremost—"eventually didn't feel so liberating, but limiting."

Instagram not only mitigates against but can also enhance feminist expression, particularly when it embraces the platform's visual features, for example, by optimizing one's self-presentation based on social signals. Feminism can help reduce inhibitions of putting oneself on display, allowing some feminist users to reap the benefits of individualistic, aspirational self-presentation more abundantly, while enabling others to pursue and communicate a feminist politics that affirms the pleasures of desire and visibility.

Minute Deviations

Maya, a student in her mid-twenties, described herself as "a typical millennial." Her pursuits and preoccupations included branding, marketing, social media, modeling, and "hair things," all of which she was trying to turn into a successful career as a freelancer. Her Instagram profile, with roughly five thousand followers, was part of that ambition. Maya's protest against fat shaming (shown in Figure 4.2) illustrates a recurring pattern we encountered when speaking to Instagram feminists. The text on her t-shirt articulates a strong critique of beauty standards and thus expresses her feminist commitments. The image itself, however, confirms those standards. This is not to say that Maya is somehow failing to be sufficiently or properly feminist. Making compromises with Instagram's visual idiom and mode of interaction is an almost inescapable part of feminist expression.

Another way Maya tried to resolve the tension between others' expectations and her need to express different sides of herself was to maintain a "finsta" (fake Instagram) account

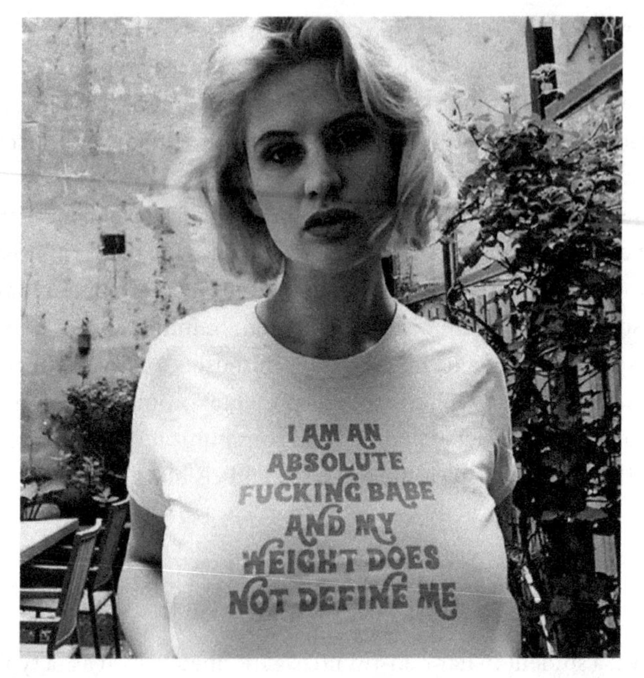

Figure 4.2 Maya's protest against fat shaming. Reproduced with permission.

featuring less polished images (see Figure 4.3). The two images in Figure 4.3 were taken on the same occasion, maybe even just seconds apart, and apparently depict the same subject matter: blue skies, rooftops, potted plants, and a young woman in a bathing suit and sunglasses, brandishing a wine bottle. But while the image that made it to Maya's main account has her poised body filling most of the frame, the finsta image has a goofier quality thanks to the splayed presence of the full length of her body bisecting the image. Maya's knees and pink slippers make the frame, negating any pretense of elegance. The differences are minute, but consequential.

Figure 4.3 Maya and her finsta. Reproduced with permission.

Erika's story provides another example of small but significant differences. She made vexing compromises to share her activist projects while maintaining her following. She tried to abstain from posting anything that "could make other people jealous, because that is such a big part of [Instagram's] business model"—but faced continuous difficulties. "Instagram is very much about individual achievements and competition in a way that is difficult to combine with feminism," she reflected. "I try to counter that, but I also see that it goes against the way the medium is created. I always get the most response and engagement on pictures of myself." Erika found this particularly challenging because of her left-wing commitments. "But then I also realize that, sometimes, to get a political message across, I have to be in the image myself . . . I struggle with Instagram as a platform a lot." Her compromise was to appear in posts, but to attempt to call attention to radical ideas and decenter herself (Figure 4.4).

Rebecca, who told us she likes to put her successful career in fashion on display, scrolled through her profile looking for "honest moments" that didn't just portray her "Insta life." While she doesn't maintain a finsta, she found a few examples in her feed, including one that showed her on the verge of tears, but then observed, "Of

Figure 4.4 Erika decentering herself. Reproduced with permission.

course, it's heavily curated still, but that's Insta." What did she mean by "curated"? "It's still pretty pictures. It's my best angle and lighting. I still look pretty in my opinion. The things that I'm insecure about, I don't post. I love my body, but would never post my fat belly," she explained. "The posts must fit the image of myself that I want to put out there. A strong woman who is a powerhouse in work, that is pretty but not fake and that is funny and has a fun life." She showed us an image taken just seconds after one she had posted which showed half her face up close, with teary eyes and splotchy skin. "I didn't post it because I don't want people to think I'm mentally unstable or asking for attention."

These stories highlight a key paradox facing Instagram feminists. They do considerable work to produce *minute deviations* from the prevailing standards of decorum and display on Instagram. The subtlety of these deviations was often such that we wouldn't have spotted them had interviewees not pointed them out as such. "Honest" or "real life" posts, much as they purport to "keep it real," do little to disrupt the ground rules. In fact, they ultimately serve to validate and uphold the rules by paying a conflicted kind of tribute to them. Honesty and realness are themselves performances functioning as markers of distinction within the established visual vernacular.

A profile, Rebecca told us, ought to be *cur*ated, not *cre*ated. Similar demands to balance the ideal and the authentic bear on

Instagram users more generally, and this tension is a recurring theme in the social psychological literature on social media (Davis 2014). The demand for authenticity arguably has a special resonance for feminists because feminist sensibilities often manifest as a desire to be radically honest. Such an ethic demands not being "fake" or contorting oneself in pursuit of an unattainable ideal.

To bring the pushes and pulls that condition filtering and engender minute deviations into even sharper relief, it is instructive to consider Nika's story. A student and fashion designer in their late twenties, Nika was the only person we interviewed who sought to pursue alternatives without compromise. They embraced a "poor" look—both in terms of the outfits they depicted on Instagram as well as the "bad" quality of the images they posted (Figure 4.5). This was a rare use of *counter-aesthetics*, motivated by their anticapitalist ideology. "I want to break this idea of what a stylish, fashionable person is," Nika told us. "I make an effort to look like a bum. And I think more people should do that. Because then people would respect each other more based on humanity than on looks." And it takes considerable effort. Nika explained they must "*try* to be really proud" of their bad quality photos and Stories, but at the same time, "I feel this pressure about my presence. I feel the need for my account to look like an artist's account." Knowing that their images may not be catchy enough, and that even their friends had

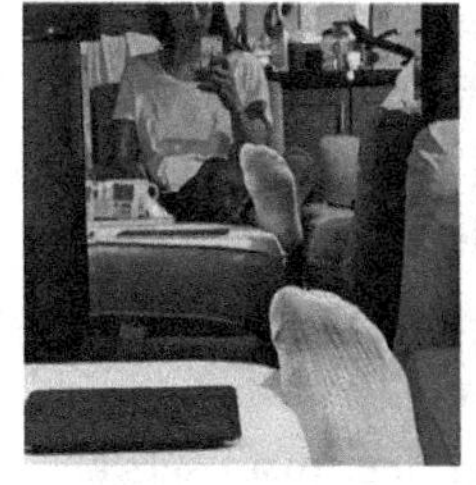

Figure 4.5 Nika's counter-aesthetics. Reproduced with permission.

stopped paying attention, it was an ongoing struggle to resist the alluring social and economic rewards promised by Instagram.

Many interviewees who expressed frustration with Instagram became more passive about updating their profiles instead of challenging how social reward is typically distributed on the platform on evidence of social, professional, or aesthetic accomplishment. Even if users were to choose such a radical course of action, as Nika did, they run the risk that their actions would be construed as yet another thirsty quest for status.

Most feminist users therefore make compromises most of the time; their posts conform to Instagram's ground rules, but contain minute deviations that offer a small window into alternative ways of being and seeing (see also Caldeira, De Ridder, and Van Bauwel 2020). Often, this results in posts that may not *look* very different, but that *feel* different. Images with the right vibe serve to authenticate the presentation of self, even if their polish and allure mean they can blend in with Instagram's dominant aesthetic mode.

Conclusion

Feminisms of varying positions of compliance and resistance vis-à-vis the status quo struggle for visibility on the terrain of popular culture (Banet-Weiser 2018). The tension between compliance and resistance that characterizes competing feminist visibilities on social media plays out not only *between* but also *within* feminists, as they strategically conceal, amplify, or adjust aspects of their selves. In concert with algorithmic feedback loops, the filtering practices that Instagram users adopt shape emerging feminist visibilities, producing feminist imagery that strategically *evades* feminist issues that sit uneasily with the platform's interaction order. At the same time, Instagram also *amplifies* feminist expressions and self-projects, as the constant feedback between feminist users and their audiences boosts issues that resonate widely, like individual empowerment and sex-positivity. But even in its amplificatory mode, Instagram feminism remains tightly within the confines of audience acceptance and interest. It is ambiguous to the core: feminist posts make claims to transgressiveness and resistance, while in their form and content they seek to accommodate the platform's cross-pressures. More often than not, the polished surfaces of feminist Instagram profiles hide ideological rifts and personal struggles.

When faced with these conflicting tugs and pulls, feminist Instagram users make vexing compromises. They adopt the strategy of minute deviations, keeping their aspirational self and the social capital of their curated profile intact while mounting a subdued challenge to gendered ideals and norms. It is no wonder, then, that Instagram feminists have not developed a widely shared critical account of the relational and aesthetic labor demanded by self-branding or the competitive drive behind interactions on Instagram. Subdued as they are, minute deviations do not stir controversy and do not amount to a direct assault on patriarchal and sexist norms. Then again, these deviations are meaningful and resonant to those who express them, reaffirming their identity as feminists. And while minute deviations do not represent a concerted or overt challenge, they do incrementally and partially shift social norms. By assimilating feminism into Instagrammism, feminism diffuses and becomes part of "the visual zeitgeist" (Leaver, Highfield, and Abidin 2020, 216). Whether this change should be considered lamentable, insignificant, meaningful, or even revolutionary depends on one's political outlook. What is sure, though, is that feminist visibilities are transformed in the process. This serves to amplify feminisms that stress individual autonomy, success, beauty, and confidence while offering less space for structural critique, collective action, emotional distress, and ambivalence.

5

Integration and Conformity

Upon entering De Trut, visitors must agree with the bar's house rules. Apart from the usual warnings—don't disturb the neighbors and follow the instructions of personnel—De Trut has a strict ban on phones and cameras. Why? On its website, the bar provides the following explanation:

> Because we find it unpleasant and anti-social when people are making calls, sending text messages, or using Facebook or Twitter all the time . . . . But also because every phone has a camera . . . We want to be a safe space by and for dikes, trans, and fags, regardless of who you are and where you're heading. It should not be taken for granted that someone who visits De Trut is out. That's why we absolutely don't want people making photographs or recordings.

De Trut ("The Bitch") was founded in 1985 in the heyday of Amsterdam's squatting movement. The movement was, in some respects, decidedly patriarchal: domineering men were the informal leaders of the movement, and during the frequent confrontations with riot police they commanded movement participants in much the same way that officers lead their battalions. But there was also a powerful counter-current of squatters who wanted to break free from inherited gender and sexual roles. Many squat bars created what are now called "safe spaces" for gays, lesbian, drags, trans, and queer people to socialize and party without the suffocating heteronormative gaze that governs mainstream establishments. De Trut is among the few places that remain from the 1980s wave of activism and stands as a monument of radical left queer subculture.

On Display. John D. Boy and Justus Uitermark, Oxford University Press. © Oxford University Press 2024.
DOI: 10.1093/oso/9780197629437.003.0005

For this subculture to survive and thrive it must close itself off from the mainstream and reduce its visibility. The possibility that what happens in the space will be recorded and circulated is threatening and paralyzing.[1] While the ban on cameras is instrumental to creating a safe space, it also means that De Trut relies almost entirely on word-of-mouth for attracting visitors, making it hard for queer youth, recent arrivals to the city, or others who rely on social media and digital platforms for wayfinding to spot the place. First-time visitors writing Google reviews generally love the place, not least because of the ban on phones. At the same time, they perceive it as "very local" and "very exclusive," not as particularly welcoming.

While De Trut would shrivel if exposed to the limelight of social media, other places thrive in it. Bars, clubs, restaurants, boutiques, and even upscale supermarkets routinely nudge customers to take pictures and circulate them on social media. Coffee & Coconuts is a shining example. The place radiates Instagrammability. A former theater, the place features the minimalist interior design that has become the hallmark of cosmopolitan café culture—white-washed walls, iron beams, wooden tables. Small touches like palm trees and murals of surfers set it apart by creating a tropical vibe, and vertical sight lines through the cavernous space provide opportunities for stunning photographs. Coffee & Coconuts employs a marketing specialist, but most of the promotional work is done by customers. Every day, dozens of customers post pictures of themselves, their food, and their coffee. Not only is the volume impressive; what is especially striking is that virtually all the images look like advertisements. The people look beautiful, young, and happy; the latte art is impeccable; and the food, particularly the full breakfast and the coconuts, looks wholesome and colorful. Coffee & Coconuts thrives on Instagram—this "Mecca for all Instagrammers," as an adoring visitor called it, attracts a bounty of adherents.

De Trut and Coffee & Coconuts are obviously very different, and so is their relation to social media. De Trut wants to provide shy or outrageous queers with a refuge from prying eyes, while Coffee & Coconuts offers a stage on which its visitors can confidently present themselves to the world. This is precisely the argument we develop in this chapter: the visibility promulgated through social media affects urban subcultures in very different ways. Subcultures centered on high-status and conformist consumption thrive, while rebellious and deviant subcultures tend to wane. The force that drives conformity is integration: social media binding people together. Social media make cities more like the court societies described by Elias (1983): people and places are tied together in dense webs of connections in which status displays are at the center.

If this is correct, it is quite different from what the literature on social media and cities would lead us to expect. There the dominant narrative is about polarization. Social media, so the argument goes, potentially provide a space for democratic deliberation (the dream of the "networked public sphere" that we discussed in Chapter 2), but in practice they serve to reinforce our differences. As they help and encourage us to associate with like-minded people, social media inadvertently yet ineluctably draw us into echo chambers. Making matters worse, algorithms reinforce our propensity to associate with those like us by suggesting we befriend our friends' friends or keep reading the blog we just visited. Social media, then, feed on our differences and reinforce them, resulting in subcultural differentiation and polarization (Pariser 2011; Sunstein 2001). As ties to people like us become stronger, the distance from others grows. We would further expect this dynamic of subcultural differentiation to be especially pronounced in cities because scholars, starting with the Chicago School of urban sociology and the Manchester School of anthropology, have argued that cities cultivate and amplify difference for over a century.

While contemporary and classical literature on cities and social media would lead us to think of both as sites of polarization, the previous chapters offered a different perspective. Drawing on Elias's relational sociology, we suggested social media link people together in chains of interdependence and insert them into unified systems of rank. Instead of dividing people into mutually closed-off echo chambers or filter bubbles that nurture subcultural idiosyncrasy and extremism, social media make their users acutely aware of what people beyond their immediate social circles might find appealing or offensive. The result is what art critic Tijmen Schep (2017) calls "social cooling": social media users averting risks and flaunting their virtue to improve their reputational scores. While in its early days the internet offered ample space for communities to construct niches and cultivate differences, the rise of digital platforms has brought the mainstream closer. This is especially true for visual and geo-locative social media like Instagram where users, their social networks, and their environments are actually or potentially on display. Difference does not so much disappear but comes to be expressed through ever more subtle and individual strategies of distinction—a process Elias (1994, 2:382–386) captures with the phrase "diminishing contrasts, increasing varieties."

This chapter examines the dynamics of subcultural integration and differentiation in Amsterdam and on Instagram through interviews and observations as well as computational analysis. For the computational analysis, we use a corpus of more than seven hundred thousand geotagged posts gathered between December 2015 and June 2016. The total number of users in our corpus is roughly equivalent to about one-tenth of Amsterdam's population. (Consult the Appendix for further details on the platform data we used and the techniques we employed to analyze it.)

To study differentiation among these users, we consider reciprocated ties (I comment on, or like, your post *and* you comment on, or like, my post). Out of the millions of interactions in our data, 130,665 were reciprocated. We ran a community detection algorithm on these mutual ties to identify groups of users that have relatively many connections among each other. We inspect these clusters to characterize them and identify the places that members of these clusters tend to tag.[2] We further rely on observations of these places and interviews with proprietors and workers, looking both at places that thrive on Instagram and places that struggle in different ways with the visibility afforded by Instagram and other social media.

Subcultural Zones at the Interface of Instagram and the City

Urban cultural scenes are grounded in sets of interlinked places that allow urban dwellers with kindred interests to meet, develop shared sensibilities, and engage in consumption practices that define their identities (Silver and Clark 2016). We call such sets of places "zones" and identify them as follows. Applying the community detection algorithm, we find a total of thirty-one clusters consisting of two hundred or more users. We list the nine largest clusters in Table 5.1 to give an impression of how Instagram users in Amsterdam sort into different groups based on their backgrounds and preferences, but we use all thirty-one clusters in the analyses that follow.[3] We inspect place tags to map the zones. When users within the same clusters tag places, we see those places as linked.[4]

We construct a proximity matrix of places based on how frequently they are tagged by people in the same cluster. We then apply the same method of community detection as discussed above to identify zones, first turning the proximity matrix into a weighted co-occurrence network. This yields four zones. Table 5.2 presents an overview of the four zones and some additional data on the places that we sourced from Yelp, the popular social reviews site.[5] Before considering in greater detail how these zones and the places that make them up are bound up with status displays in the city, we first describe their features.

Table 5.1 The Nine Largest Clusters of Instagram Users

#	Label	Users	Posts	Median Number of Followers
1	City Consumers	4,642	86,925	684
2	Hedonist Lifestyles	4,412	57,879	785
3	City Imageers	3,977	81,482	562
4	Rich Kids	3,196	20,225	552
5	Gay Performers	2,843	31,904	550
6	Refined Lifestyles	2,097	33,682	857
7	Clubbing	2,073	22,234	707
8	Beliebers	1,952	11,740	498
9	Fitness	1,773	23,301	520

The *nightlife zone* consists, at its core, of places associated with the city's clubbing scenes. According to Yelp, a typical closing time for places in the nightlife zone is 6 a.m. Concert venues, like Paradiso and Melkweg, and clubs, like Jimmy Woo, Bitterzoet, and Club Air, are at the center. Generally, we find most of the city's dance clubs and a high number of bars and cafés within this zone. Footwear and sportswear stores carrying local brands also rank highly, suggesting that certain sartorial styles predominate in the city's clubbing scenes and serve as a source of subcultural capital (Thornton 1996). Images tend to show performers and groups swept up in the action. More than in any other zone, the images taken here show moments of collective enjoyment.

If the nightlife zone is about dancing, the *lifestyle zone* appears to be about eating. The young urban professional's favorite meal, brunch, is an important occasion to frequent places in this zone, in which hotels, cafés, and restaurants that serve brunch staples, like poached eggs and pancakes, predominate. At the center of this

Table 5.2 Zones at the Interface of the City and Instagram

	Nightlife	Lifestyle	Culture	Fitness
Tagged Places	604	588	533	91
Average Latest Closing Time	6:00 a.m.	6:00 p.m.	5:00 p.m.	6:30 p.m.
Most Common Hashtags	#music #party #paradiso	#food #love #coffee	#rijksmuseum #netherlands #iamsterdam	#fitness #workout #gym
Posts	71,312	49,431	42,151	10,976
Users	19,912	13,085	15,648	3,945
Focal Areas	Leidseplein, Rembrandtplein	Herengracht, De Pijp	Museumplein, Amsterdam Arena	Zuid, Noord
Standout Places	Paradiso, Jimmy Woo	The Hoxton, Conservatorium Hotel	Rijksmuseum, Eye Film Museum	Changing Life Hub, Vondel Gym
Typical Images	Bands, performers, dancing	Food, clothes, group shots, selfies	Art, architecture, outside views	Groups, action shots, selfies, outfits

zone, we find a number of upmarket hotels—the Conservatorium, The Hoxton, and W Hotel—where patrons like to photograph beautifully plated French toast and bespoke cocktails. Boutique coffee places, such as the aforementioned Coffee & Coconuts, as well as a slew of restaurants serving various cuisines, also form part of this zone. Several locations on the city's luxury shopping street, the P.C. Hooftstraat, are also among the lifestyle locations, as are other places associated with fashion and design, such as the Dutch headquarters of Hearst, publishers of *Elle*, *Harper's Bazaar*, *Esquire*, and *Cosmopolitan*; a showroom of Dutch design; and a fashion retailer specializing in "the good things in life." Looking again at Yelp reviews, places in this zone stand out for both their high ratings and their high prices.[6] Images foreground moments of consumption, often conspicuous, or at least indicative of an omnivorous sophistication (Veblen 1934; Currid-Halkett 2017).

The *cultural zone* revolves around the city's museums, with the iconic Rijksmuseum at the helm. Alongside it are other well-known landmarks and cultural institutions—the zoo, botanical garden, and the opera house, as well as the public library's central branch—which are frequented by the city's cultural connoisseurs and pictured for distant audiences who appreciate images of Amsterdam cityscapes and sights. Users tagging these locations frequently invoke the city brand #iamsterdam, which in its sculpture form was an inescapable sight on Instagram serving as a metonymy for the city as a whole (which lacks instantly recognizable landmarks on par with the Eiffel Tower or Big Ben). These locations are often tagged by people with a more international audience, such as international students and expats, suggesting they signal well to these international audiences as markers of being in Amsterdam.

Finally, the smallest of the four is the *fitness zone*, which unsurprisingly revolves around sports clubs and gyms. Amsterdam's CrossFit gyms and yoga studios can be found in this zone, along with Yoghurt Barn franchises. This zone comprises not only places appealing to the health-conscious, but also establishments that cater to other practices involving the body, such as tattoo parlors and a cryotherapy center (where customers can subject their bodies to temperatures of −110 degrees Celsius for three minutes). More than in other zones, the ideal of expressive individualism (Turner 2011) shines through in the displays from this zone.

The uneven presence of clusters in different territories supports the assumption that places are used strategically for displays that play to different social scenes, garnering rewards in the form of esteem or recognition. The fitness zone stands out as the preferred domain of several clusters revolving around fitness and tattooing, suggesting that esteem in these groups is bound up with particular places and what they afford—in this case, getting and maintaining an attractive, fit, and healthy body. The three larger zones, which revolve around nightlife, culture, and lifestyle, also show clear, albeit less pronounced, tendencies. Nightlife locations are tagged by users in the Hedonist Lifestyles cluster and the Clubbing cluster, while locations in the culture zone are tagged by the City Imageers cluster, as well as internationally oriented clusters of expats and foreign-exchange students. Lifestyle locations are tagged by various clusters of apparel and fashion enthusiasts. Unsurprisingly, we also find the users from the Refined Lifestyles cluster represented here.

This aspirational dimension of Instagram use comes out not only in the places that are tagged but also in what is portrayed in these places and how. We could start with the most notorious genre of social media post—the selfie. Generally, commentary on the selfie is out of proportion to its actual prominence on most social media (Caliandro and Graham 2020), and in our data, too, selfies account for only a small proportion of the total volume. In the fitness zone, however, posts bearing a #selfie hashtag (or ironic variations like #shamelessgymselfie) can be found far more frequently, which speaks to the centrality of the physical self to status displays staged in this zone.[7] In the culture zone, architectural details and outside views predominate because here recognition hinges on one's identification with the branded image of Amsterdam. In the lifestyle zone, bands, performers, and party people literally take center stage—here esteem is rewarded on evidence of hedonistic pursuits. Unlike in the selfie-saturated fitness zone, portraits are more likely to show groups than individuals. Finally, in the lifestyle zone, still lifes of desirable items—especially food, fashion, and furniture—speak to the ways in which conspicuous consumption continues to be an avenue toward prestige.

In short, by combining community detection with geographic analysis, we can show how subcultural groups use digital technologies to mark their territory within the city. This suggests that differentiation occurs not only through residential segregation, but also through more complex sorting processes taking place on the interface of social media and the city (Graham 2005; Wang et al. 2018).

Integration on the Interface of Instagram and the City

As our analysis in this chapter has so far illustrated, we do indeed find subcultural differentiation on the interface of Instagram and the city in the sense that we can discern different communities and zones. This dovetails with the large literature we mentioned above that directs our attention to divisions online and in the city. But the Eliasian perspective we developed in Chapter 2 prompts us to also look for countervailing tendencies. An important part of our argument is that Instagram and other social media help foster integration and conformity. Whether we find that one or the other tendency—toward integration and conformity or toward separation and differentiation—prevails will depend in large part on the instruments that we use. So far, we followed the lead of other researchers in applying community detection to identify groups and characterizing clusters according to their most central nodes. We thus found what we were looking for: differences between clusters. But we could also look differently. Had we looked at random users, it would have been much harder to characterize clusters. For example, many (but *not all*) users in the cluster of "gay performers" might present as gay or performers, but gay folks and performers are also to be found in other clusters. What is true for community detection also holds for our strategy of identifying zones: it is a method designed to highlight differences by filtering out similarity. We need to look more closely, and we may also need to look differently, if we want to bring integration and conformity into view. We do this by first taking a very coarse-grained view of the location of clusters within the city before zooming in on their linkages and shared spaces.

When we look at the spatial footprint of the different clusters, as we do in Figure 5.1, we get a different sense of how Instagram users are positioned within the city. What is remarkable is that the heat maps are so much alike: all clusters have their center of gravity in the center of the city. There are a couple of clusters that also show a lot of activity in Amsterdam South East because of the concert venues in that neighborhood, but this is hardly distinctive. If there is one cluster that stands out, it is a cluster with Amsterdammers of Turkish descent (Cluster 16) that shows a lot of activity in the Western part of the city. However, this cluster, too, gravitates to the center of the city. While both classic writings on the city and contemporary writing on social media would lead us to expect stark differences, we do not at all find that groups sort into internally homogeneous enclaves or "natural areas."

One might counter that the maps in Figure 5.1 are not at the right scale. Perhaps different clusters all tend to post from the city center but from different places within it. The mixing of different groups in the city center would, in this scenario, conceal profound processes of segregation operating at a lower scale where people might keep out others by constructing a parochial realm (Lofland 1998). Even though members of different clusters traverse the same spaces in the city's center, they might ultimately self-segregate into different places—a pattern referred to in the literature as "social tectonics" (Butler and Robson 2001; Jackson and Butler 2015). When analyzing at the level of the places, we do not find strong support for this scenario. If we look at the one hundred places that are tagged the most (in at least 309 posts), we find not a single place where posts originate from one cluster only. It is very common for places to be frequented by members of multiple communities. As

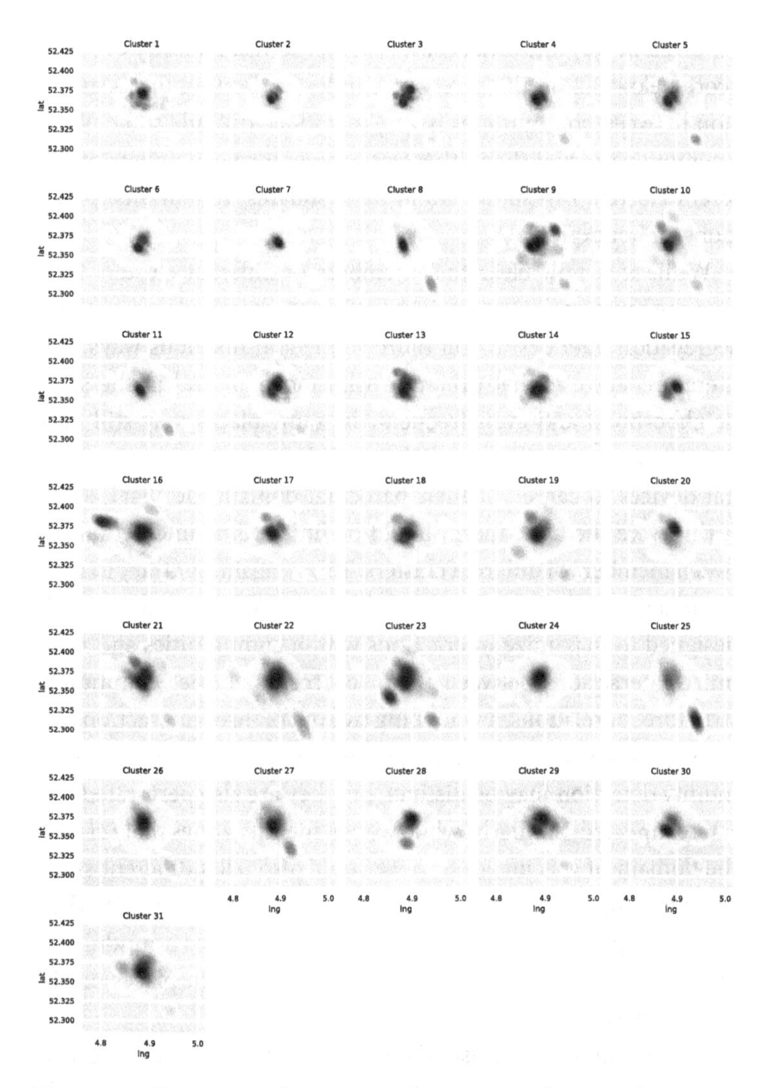

Figure 5.1 Heat maps of Instagram activity around Amsterdam for different groups. Each map is centered on the same coordinates. Hotter colors indicate more place tags. *Note*: The place tag and the location from which a message is posted do not necessarily coincide—a user may append a place tag for "Club Vividio" while posting from their homes.

reported in Boy and Uitermark (2016), the vast majority of places score below 0.2 on the divergence index, indicating that segregation between communities is very low indeed. While some places are more parochial than others, as a general rule members of different clusters rub shoulders in bars, squares, restaurants, parks, clubs, or boutiques.

While it is now clear that members of different clusters traverse the same spaces and rub shoulders in shared places, perhaps segregation operates in still more subtle and insidious ways. The literature suggests that urbanites who move around in the same neighborhood and even frequent the same places may still have little to no contact. They may "live together apart" as they use digital devices to carve out their parochial domain (de Waal 2014). If this were the case, there should be little online interaction between members of different clusters. This is, again, contrary to what we actually find. Although the community detection algorithm is designed to maximize interactions within communities and minimize interactions between them to accentuate the "community structure" of relations, a whopping two out of three interactions are between, not within, clusters. The clusters observed through community detection may be distinct, but they are also perforated and interconnected. Similarly, while we can identify zones that serve as the domain of specific groups, we could also tell a different story. The place network—where different places are connected when they are tagged by people in the same cluster—has a modularity of only 0.15, indicating many connections between places of different zones.

The communities Amsterdam Instagrammers spawn are neither bubbles nor bounded fields, and interactions frequently span across clusters. Amsterdam Instagrammers organize into clusters according to their lifestyles and backgrounds but neither on Instagram nor in the places they tag are they far removed from others. People may have a primary reference group that is most consequential for how they understand and comport themselves, but this primary reference group is not split off from the rest of the social world. While they associate with people with similar interests and lifestyles, they generally do not form enclaves. On social media, strangers are never far away and our audiences are always multiple, at least potentially (Marwick and Boyd 2010).[8] These findings support the hypothesis derived from Elias that social media extend and intensify linkages across social groups, bringing them into each other's purview.

Closure and Visibility

Networks enabled by social media incorporate different groups and places into a grid of visibility. But how, exactly, are places materially affected by this incorporation? To answer this question, we talked to proprietors and social media managers of different places in the zones identified above. We covered both places that are at the very center of Instagram networks as well as places that are less prominent. While journalistic accounts often focus on places that are designed to be Instagram magnets (e.g., Chayka 2016; Matchar 2017; CityLab Staff 2017), in most places the impact of Instagram is more subtle and complex. Proprietors and visitors strategically respond to social media depending on how much they can and want to align with prevailing norms.

For some places, social media attention is an unqualified good. Coffee & Coconuts is literally designed to be "Instagrammable," and its customers act on cue by posting food close-ups and manicured selfies. There is a seamless feedback loop between online and on-site, nobody must make difficult choices or engage in soul-searching. The same is true for Chicago Social Club and Jimmy Woo, two renowned night clubs. Rolf, an associate at the firm that manages social media on their behalf, explained how he figured out whom to recruit for his campaigns. He found the men by looking closely at what happened around the dance floor. "There are always one or two guys in a club to whom others defer. People come to those guys to show respect, shaking their hand. It's a guy thing, showing who you are and who you know, sort of mafia-like. It's a struggle for dominance, a crossing of horns." Once he had figured out who the alpha males were, he recruited them as influencers. "Men are the decision-makers, so once you have them on board, the women will follow." But he explained that women are important, too, especially online. Rolf believed that women use Instagram more frequently, and he adjusted his content accordingly, posting many pictures of women having fun. "Women like to look at women, and men like to look at women too." Finding the right people and choreographing the right images is a craft, but to Rolf it was obvious what was "right": he was picturing beautiful young women and attractive alpha males. Circulating more of those images brought in more of those people—a smooth feedback loop.

Other places have a more ambiguous relation with Instagram's visual culture, even some places that gain a big share of Instagram attention. The Vondel Gym is probably the best-known fitness club in the Netherlands, on equal footing in terms of prestige to Jimmy Woo. We see this reflected in our data: the gym towers above others in terms of the attention it commands on Instagram. But for its proprietors this is not an unqualified good. Pictures tagged #vondelgym often feature men showing off six-pack abs and women doing squats to tone their buttocks, but Luna, the proprietor, envisioned a different kind of gym. She wanted to build an inclusive community in her gym, and one way to achieve this was to curate the gym's Instagram feed to feature greater diversity in terms of age, skin color, and gender expression. She also actively discouraged what she referred to as "fit fascists," who show off their bodies and claim superior fitness knowledge, going so far as to ask them to leave the premises when they made recordings. Luna paid special attention to what she referred to as "non-normative" people from groups who are shunned in other gyms. For instance, she organized training sessions especially for fat people and for trans people.

While the Vondel Gym was in the core of the fitness zone, it resisted conforming to the aesthetic and ethic that prevailed there. The gym deliberately used its status—owed to the fame of its founder, as well as the raw industrial aesthetics of its building—to push back against the mainstream norms around fitness and beauty that prevail in other gyms and on Instagram. Whether this attempt was successful or not is a matter of perception and opinion: the online representations of Vondel Gym are noticeably, but not radically, different from those of other gyms. Despite Luna's best efforts, the deviations are minute; the #shamelessgymselfie aesthetic prevails.

Marieke worked in webcare at the popular Van Gogh Museum. In Dutch organizations, "webcare" refers to the work of responding to queries and complaints received through social media channels. Like Luna, Marieke had an ambivalent relation to social media. She knew that posts of famous paintings, like the *Sunflowers* or *The Potato Eaters*, would generate high engagement, but she felt like that would be too easy. While on an organizational chart a "webcare worker" is a mid-level bureaucrat within a sprawling institution, this was not how Marieke approached her job. She did not have the prestigious title of "curator," but Marieke's digital curation was hugely consequential for what people saw of the Van Gogh Museum. At the time, the Museum had 2.5 million followers on Facebook and 1.7 million followers on Instagram, giving Marieke a huge reach. Because the Museum did not need to make an effort to attract visitors—it is permanently at capacity—Marieke used the museum's social media channels for what she called "educational purposes." She was not so interested in posting nice pictures (although she noticed that paintings with sharp color contrasts work especially well), but provided background stories, gave explanations about Van Gogh's style of using complementary colors, and drew attention to some of the museum's lesser known items, like the letters between Vincent and his brother Theo. Marieke resisted the lure of maximizing likes and follower counts to cultivate a community of international Van Gogh enthusiasts.

Both the Vondel Gym and the Van Gogh Museum have very strong reputations and are exceptionally prominent online. They can *afford* to resist the siren call of Instafame. Most other places are not so lucky. Whereas the success of the Van Gogh Museum makes it possible to extend and deepen engagement with the oeuvre of the famous painter, the Eye Film Museum is in a more conflicted position. Not that things are going badly. The museum's futuristic new building in Amsterdam Noord has become an icon with a strong Instagram presence, and the team managing the Dutch film museum's social media accounts knows it can count on posters featuring internationally popular actors and movies to generate engagement. Deborah, the content creator for the museum we briefly discussed in the introduction, told us that these victories have proven double-edged. The success has put the Eye on the map but it has created tensions within the organization. Gradually, the Eye as architectural icon and receptacle of Hollywood references has pushed to the side the museum's original mission of archiving Dutch film. Because the Eye Film Museum, unlike other cultural institutions in Amsterdam, must work hard to attract visitors, Deborah wanted to have a more informal and slick style of communication—"we've been too high-brow, too formal"—optimized for engagement. In practice, this meant reinforcing a process where archives and historical artefacts are progressively removed from view, both online and on-site. Social media here do not serve to develop a community around the museum, but they reflect and fuel a trend of popularization.

Something similar is true for Monk, an indoor climbing and bouldering gym. To attract different kinds of customers than the more traditional indoors climbing spots, Monk tried out a different approach. They installed a DJ booth and opened a bar serving fresh juices and craft beers. "We wanted to become a place that people would visit before going to a club," Remco, one of the owners, explained. The holds are brightly colored, and the wall is painted in pastel, offering the sort of color contrast that works so well in Instagram posts. The makeover was a success: the number of visitors exploded. It is impossible to say to what extent social media contributed to this success, but it certainly played a role. Monk thrived online, in contrast to Amsterdam's more old-fashioned climbing spots. Visitors shared images of their first forays into climbing, injecting a stream of promotional material into peer networks. But there was also a cost to the success. The community of fanatical climbers that had grown around Monk felt like they were losing the space to the flock of incidental visitors who came to hang out rather than to climb the boulder circuits. Monk's solution was to cede its main gym hall to the new mainstream and create a separate spot, Club Monk, for the community of devoted climbers. Club Monk doesn't offer rental shoes or courses, nor does it have a bar. All design decisions are part of a deliberate effort to shield the bouldering community from the mainstream. Everything is functional, crude in an industrial way, although not in the ironically brutalist sense that Instagrammers appreciate. Although Monk cherishes its community of devoted climbers sufficiently to want to accommodate them, it now does so in a more peripheral and smaller location.

All these places feel the pressure to conform. Instagram appears, to them, as a vehicle of hegemonic gender norms, prevailing beauty standards, and, more specifically, Instagram's aesthetic requirements of bright lights and bold contrasts. This does not pose a problem for places and people that can readily conform to the standards. If you want to be the kind of place where people can "see and be seen," like Jimmy Woo and Coffee & Coconuts, permeation by social media isn't a problem. For other places, it is more confounding. Places like the Van Gogh Museum and the Vondel Gym cope with the pressure by carving out spaces for people and practices that don't easily find a home otherwise. Yet other places, like the Eye Film Museum and the bouldering gym Monk, change their profiles, grudgingly or enthusiastically deprioritizing some of the things and people that previously defined them. Finally, the pressure to conform is felt most intensely in places and by people that are at risk of overexposure. De Trut is an example, but it is not the only place where phones have been banned altogether. De School, a dance club, also banned phones because they undermined its ambition to be an "inclusive" club—the phones had the effect that people were playing it safe, not acting or dressing out of the ordinary. To the extent that difference requires a buffer against the mainstream to flourish, the presence of phones and visibility on social media networks serve as panoptic devices of normalization.

As social media engulf cities, their residents respond. Places develop different strategies to optimize, harness, channel, or thwart social media visibility. Central to these strategies is the tension between optimizing for social media engagement by appealing to distant audiences versus cultivating a distinct community locally. Places assemble different kinds of communities—of art lovers, queers, or boulderers—but their attempts invariably involve resisting the mainstream gaze that is carried by Instagram and other social media. Whereas the literature predominantly views social media as amplifiers of difference by means of fragmentation, here we see how social media serves as a force for integration that moderates difference and pressures places and people to conform.

Intermezzo: A Natural Experiment

Now that we have argued why we should acknowledge Instagram's role as a vehicle of integration, let us examine another central premise underlying these analyses. If place tagging indeed represents a symbolic claim on space and a marker of status, as we contend, then privileged and resourceful groups should use place tags more than others. This expectation is difficult to test because we usually can only sample on the dependent variable. We know who tags places because doing so leaves a digital trace, but we lack data on who does not use the feature. However, thanks to a quirk in our data, we were able to perform a natural experiment of sorts.

When Instagrammers tap "Add a Location" right before choosing to post, they can pick places from a list of predefined locations. But until August 18, 2015, there was another way for users to associate their pictures with locations. Until that date, the app had an additional button, mysteriously named "Add to Photo Map." This feature was introduced in version 3.0 of the Instagram app, which launched in 2012, a few months after the acquisition by Facebook (now Meta). In this version of the interface, users that wanted to tag a location first had to tap this button before *optionally* selecting the predefined location from a list or entering their own location name. If users only tapped "Add to Photo Map" but did not select a location, the metadata associated with their posts would include rooftop coordinates, but the named location field would be blank. This was a confusing feature for many, as several interviews we conducted with Instagram users prior to the interface change revealed. In addition, once toggled on, "Add to Photo Map" would remain on. None of our interviewees consciously used the feature.

This quirk in our data therefore allows us to compare two sets of geotagged post: one set includes posts with locations that users consciously and conspicuously wanted to let their followers know about, and the other set includes posts with locations that users accidentally revealed. This means we can compare the differences between locations that are mentioned as part of status displays with locations that are mentioned without such a purpose. This is not a perfect natural experiment—it could be that there are users who *did* consciously share their posts' location in the photo map or it could be that only specific types of users had an interest in the photo map, etc., but that only makes it more remarkable if we do find stark differences.

Comparing posts posted two weeks before and two weeks after the interface change, we started out simply comparing what proportion of posts came from which Amsterdam neighborhood before and after the interface change. Even before the interface changed, the distribution of posts between neighborhoods was uneven. Just the two neighborhoods making up the city center accounted for more than thirty percent of all posts, while only accounting for one-tenth of the city population. On the opposite extreme, the mostly residential neighborhood of Noord-West accounts for four percent of the city's population, but it had less than one-half a percent of the city's Instagram posts. The interface change caused an even greater divergence. The two central neighborhoods now account for over forty-five percent of posts, confirming that the historical center performs a key role as a background and marker for status displays. Other neighborhoods that saw a steep increase in the proportion of geotagged posts are mostly in the rapidly gentrifying neighborhoods surrounding the historical center, such as De Pijp. In contrast, peripheral neighborhoods drop off the map almost completely. The ten neighborhoods with the smallest share of total posts account for less than seven percent (down from eighteen percent), even though forty percent of the city's population lives there. Residents of these neighborhoods previously geotagged posts from their homes or immediate surroundings, but after the interface change, when location sharing became a more conscious choice, they no longer opted to do so. Apparently, users felt no particular pride or recognized no symbolic value in the locations in these areas.

The virtual disappearance of these areas from the Instagram map renders not only places in these areas invisible, but also groups. We find that a group of street culture and hip-hop enthusiasts virtually disappeared from our dataset of geotagged posts. This was the only large cluster composed mainly of people of color, and it had a strong presence in Amsterdam's South-East borough. Before the switch, this group appended a place tag to only six percent of their posts, compared to twenty to thirty percent for other large groups (Boy and Uitermark 2017, 620). After the switch, more than four-fifths of this group no longer appears in our data, giving a strong hint that they lack places they can frequent and want to be seen in.

These findings align with those of Lindell, Jansson, and Fast (2021, 12–13), who, on the basis of survey data, observe that "the capital rich not only visit art exhibits, museums, nature reserves, conferences and theaters more frequently; they also seem inclined to expose and broadcast these visits" and conclude that geolocated platforms "constitute yet another toolset for cultural distinction and as such provide new means for cementing pre-existing class divisions." Leszczynski and Kong (2022, 1) view geolocated posts as expressions of digital spatial capital, that is, "the ability to stake claims to space through engagements with digital technology." If the city is a resource for those engaged in aspirational production (Marwick 2013, 206–207), then uneven access to different parts of the city translates into differential opportunities to attain and display status. Some groups have greater symbolic and spending power, allowing them to outshine others. Social media provides a circuit for the conversion of aesthetic displays into social esteem. Conversely, stigmatized areas and groups fade into the background on the interface of Instagram and the city.

Conclusion

Both social media and the city are widely seen as spaces of subcultural differentiation. In these spaces, commentators expect and fear that people will flock to each other, forming enclaves or bubbles, losing touch with the wider society. Departing from this perspective, this chapter traces the formation of groups at the interface of the city and Instagram. We indeed find that we can discern distinct groups around specific foci like hobbies, professions, or lifestyles. We further identify distinct zones: sets of places that serve as the domain for particular kinds of groups. People use Instagram to showcase their presence and boost their status, affirming that they belong to those places and that those places belong to them. And yet, that is not the whole story. Our findings do not conform to the dystopian image of deep and algorithmically fortified divisions. Even when users socialize in a community of CrossFit fanatics, they are never far from users with other interests, such as Beliebers or coffee aficionados. Users coalesce into groups, so much is true, but the boundaries of such groups are fuzzy. This casts social media in a different light, as vehicles of integration. Integration, in turn, results in pressure to conform.

Yes, there are radical or outlandish views on social media, even on Instagram, but there are also powerful pressures toward conformity that render countercultures precarious. In this chapter, we brought into view the wider set of relations through which norms are maintained: the fine-grained and cross-cutting linkages within and between communities. The sorts of countercultural communities discussed at the beginning of this chapter require a degree of closure to shield its members from the dominant gaze and have low chances of survival within this constellation of fine-grained and cross-cutting linkages.[9] Our findings suggest that none of the geotagged places are exclusive to a particular group. All of them, consequently, are entangled in a tightly woven web of visibility. Some places flourish under these conditions, others struggle to adapt. Others still resist exposure altogether. For them, one drastic option remains: banning phones and cameras.

6

Staging Status

Sitting on the terrace of one of his favorite restaurants, Derek, a thirty-year old marketing professional, boasted about the recent opening of new bars and restaurants in Amsterdam Oost, the city's eastern borough where he lives.[1] "It might be hard to believe, but it felt like a victory to me when the Biertuin bar opened. Suddenly my friends wanted to go out for drinks in Oost, while before, I had to cross town to meet them." Alongside his day job in marketing, Derek maintained a blog, a Facebook Page, and an Instagram account where he posted about new bars and restaurants in Amsterdam Oost. In response to the proliferation of blogs on healthy eating, he specialized in cuisines that are heavy on meat, stews and pastries. His Instagram feed is full of pictures of juicy steaks, artisan fries, and craft beers. "Oost got started a bit later than West," Derek explained, referring to the rival borough in the west. He thought things were finally kicking off, "and when something gets going, it is nice to write about it." His friends traveling across town to go out in Oost validated his decision to buy an apartment in this part of town. Derek's efforts to promote new establishments were paying off.

Derek's mediated engagements with his neighborhood illustrate how digital technologies shape and enrich the experience of place (Halegoua 2020). But they also show that perceptions and representations come to figure in a—mostly implicit but occasionally overt—struggle over what parts of the city are made visible and valued. Derek's posts from around his neighborhood are a conscious effort to boost Oost's status and, by implication, Derek's own. We see a recursive process at work: social media users selectively

On Display. John D. Boy and Justus Uitermark, Oxford University Press. © Oxford University Press 2024.
DOI: 10.1093/oso/9780197629437.003.0006

and creatively reassemble the city as they use specific places in the city as stages for their posts and these posts, in turn, become operative in changing how the city is perceived and shaped. For deeper insight into this recursive process, we focus on a single shopping street in Amsterdam Oost called Javastraat. Through this case study we want to understand how the online activities of people like Derek selectively represent *and* shape this street. The city is recomposed—cropped, filtered, tuned up, or toned down—using Instagram.

Focusing on Javastraat is a strategic choice if we want to understand how social media are implicated in urban development. Javastraat is the main shopping street in Amsterdam Oost's Indische Buurt ("Indonesian Quarter"). Built early in the twentieth century, its sizable proportion of social housing and proximity to the eastern harbor contributed to its working-class character. Following the suburbanization of many Dutch working-class and middle-class residents and the arrival of international migrants, Indische Buurt became a multicultural working-class neighborhood in the 1970s and 1980s, with ethnic minorities constituting roughly half of the population. The transformation of the Javastraat retail landscape was even more profound. While a handful of traditional Dutch stores—including a fishmonger and traditional "brown bar" (working-class pub)—have remained to this day, a large number of immigrant-run stores—including greengrocers, restaurants, phone shops, butchers, furniture stores, and a jewelry store—opened up. In the 1990s and 2000s, the street attracted customers from far and wide because of its low prices and niche ethnic products (Schoemaker 2017; Smit 2017). However, from the perspective of government officials and media commentators, Javastraat mainly bred crime and was a stain on the entire neighborhood. In 2008, the local government commissioned the refurbishment of Javastraat. As part of this upgrading, the government provided licenses to entrepreneurs it considered "bona fide."

As a result of these policy measures, and the broader process of gentrification they helped set in motion, cafés, restaurants, and designer clothing stores have proliferated. The racial and class dimensions of this process are obvious: the new establishments are mostly operated by and geared to white gentrifiers, while immigrant-run establishments mostly serve working-class ethnic minorities. While the changes in the street have been profound, the process of gentrification is even more pronounced online. Immigrant-run stores still have a strong presence in the street, but they are virtually absent online. The new establishments, in contrast, dominate social media, review sites, and blogs. Instagram users post selfies or food close-ups, reviewers on Google Maps, TripAdvisor, and Yelp talk about their experiences in the new restaurants and coffee bars, and city marketing professionals brand the street as a culturally vibrant destination. All these representations radiate pride: people are proud to live in Oost and strongly identify with the neighborhood. However, not all residents are equally zealous. Strikingly, as we will discuss, the people most vocal in expressing their identification with Oost in general, and Javastraat in particular, are not long-term residents, but rather the new arrivals. What motivates these people to express their affinity to the neighborhood? Which places do they post about on Instagram, and how? And what are the material consequences of these representations?

Answering these questions requires us to contextualize status displays on social media within the urban environment. The previous chapter has already prepared some of the ground by outlining how digital platforms and urban places serve as stages for status displays and zones for the formation of subcultures. Social media posts do not just ascribe *meaning* to places, but also *value*—they are a form of discursive investment.[2] Viewing social media posts in this way brings out the broader political economy in which meaning-making is situated. It directs our attention to the *labor* involved in producing representations, and to the *yield* in terms of status.

To investigate the online representation of Javastraat, we analyzed Instagram representations alongside blog posts and comments on review sites that pertained to locations on the shopping street. We further studied a selection of Instagram posts to learn about *who* posted about Javastraat, *what* they posted, and *how* they showed and wrote about the street (see Appendix). Apart from studying representations, we studied Javastraat on the ground through observations and interviews. As we—the book authors, as well as our collaborator Irene Bronsvoort—all live close to Javastraat, we have witnessed the street's gradual transformation and the opening of new shops and restaurants. Our conversations with entrepreneurs and residents who have attained a degree of online prominence gave us insight into the motivations, strategies, resources, and yields underlying uneven representations of the street. In addition, we can draw on extensive interview-based research on the development of the street carried out by others (van Eck, Hagemans, and Rath 2020; Sakızlıoğlu and Lees 2020; Zukin, Kasinitz, and Chen 2015).

No Place for Cucumbers

To investigate what specific parts of Javastraat are represented, we first looked at the locations in our corpus that are tagged ten times or more. This gives us a list of seventeen locations. The vast majority are new businesses; only two existed before the 2008 redevelopment. One of them is a Turkish restaurant, and the other a community center just off Javastraat. The most frequently tagged locations are mostly boutiques, bars, and cafés. Among them is a bar that specializes in rum cocktails and a designer clothing boutique that also serves specialty coffee. Meanwhile, the older establishments, typically run by immigrants and catering to lower-income customers, still form the majority of shops on the street, but they are rarely tagged or pictured.

Scrolling through this corpus and analyzing individual posts more closely, we find that they conform closely to the dominant Instagram aesthetic. As we saw in earlier chapters, users picturing Javastraat also take care to present their daily lives in aesthetically appealing ways (Leaver, Highfield, and Abidin 2020; Manovich 2017). Popular genres include pictures of people in bars, store interiors and products, cappuccino art, and beautifully arranged plates of food. The posts often depict a scene in one of the new establishments on Javastraat. We see people having drinks with friends or getting a new haircut. A subgenre consists of views of storefronts and pictures of Javastraat itself. Several posts depict the streetscape of Javastraat as seen from the sidewalk, often on a sunny day or with a beautiful sky overhead, while other posts depict a bird's-eye view of the street from a window or balcony of an apartment. A telling example is a post depicting a young Black man wearing brand-name streetwear and sunglasses, confidently walking down the Javastraat sidewalk toward the camera. The caption reads, "This street ma catwalk."

Although the posts are diverse, a dominant trope emerges: the showcasing of consumption. About seven out of ten posts from our sample refer to consumption practices. They include close-ups of items like coffee, cupcakes, cocktails, and ice cream cones. The establishments where such items are consumed are literally in the background, but they are nonetheless important enough to warrant a conspicuous mention through geotags or hashtags. Place is also signified in captions, which mostly contain cheerful, positive remarks that simultaneously celebrate the moment, the person writing the post, and the establishment where the picture was taken. One illustrative example is the Instagram post in Figure 6.1, in which a neighborhood resident expresses her appreciation for a new restaurant by posting a close-up of her Eggs Benedict with the caption "Love this new place" and a hashtag declaring her "love for Oost."

Neighborhood merchandise is another ubiquitous form of promoting and expressing ownership of the neighborhood.

Figure 6.1 Promoting a new restaurant in Amsterdam Oost. Reproduced with permission.

Multiple posts feature people posing in sweatshirts and t-shirts emblazoned with "Oost." Figure 6.2 shows how one Instagram user decided to celebrate their move into the borough: the new apartment key atop an Oost sweatshirt is not just a celebration of the user's good fortune, but a powerful illustration of a new resident investing in the neighborhood by practicing "elective belonging," as sociologist Mike Savage and colleagues (2005) have called it. Several brands sell clothing and canvas bags with Oost designs.

The owner of a designer clothing store on Javastraat who carries this brand of sweatshirts connects their popularity to the changes in the neighborhood. "There is a process of gentrification going on in the neighborhood, and you see that the sales are going extremely well because of it," he told a journalist for the local newspaper *Het Parool* (Smit 2016). "It appeals very much to the feeling that people have about living in the East. Of course it is still a poor

Figure 6.2 "New Home": the keys to a new apartment atop an Oost sweatshirt. This post was geotagged at Oosterpark. Reproduced with permission.

neighborhood, but you notice that a growing number of people are proud of living here."

Although most posts we looked at were from residents and customers posting incidentally, there is a class of prolific social media users who receive compensation for their representations. By far the most visible account covering Javastraat on Instagram was operated by Jill's Eastside, a small-scale advertising agency run by three women—all newcomers to the neighborhood. On their Instagram feed and their website, they posted pictures of different places on a daily basis, mostly cafés, bars, and stores. Their approach of writing solely positive messages on behalf of their alter ego resulted in selective highlighting of places in the neighborhood that appealed to people with similar tastes and lifestyles. While Jill's Eastside never misses an opportunity to profess her love for the neighborhood, this affinity did not extend to all establishments.

Specifically, the account amplified new places catering to gentrifiers while degrading others. They explained that the Javastraat was "really horrific," but that the neighborhood is now going in the right direction (quoted in Smidt 2015, 53). On the surface, the "Be local, buy local" motto with which Jill's Eastside promoted a pop-up store with local products suggests that they support *all* local entrepreneurs in the neighborhood. The pop-up store featured a selection of products from neighborhood stores, including books, delicacies, tableware, and local designer clothing. But Jill's Eastside only works for a select group of local shops on Javastraat. When we noted the absence of products from immigrant entrepreneurs, the women told us they lack "appropriate products" and wryly remarked that a pop-up store such as theirs has no place for cucumbers.

Javastraat as a Stage for Status Displays

We asked our research participants who created these various representations of Javastraat why they posted about the street and its surrounding neighborhood. This was an opportunity for many of our interlocutors to speak glowingly of the neighborhood and its redevelopment. They told us about what living in Indische Buurt meant to them. With a sparkle in their eyes, they talked about the neighborhood's many amenities, its ambiance, and its metropolitan and multicultural character. Most of them had moved to the neighborhood only recently, yet they strongly identified with Indische Buurt, or the borough of Oost as a whole, and did not expect to leave soon. They cited lifestyle choices and emotions, rather than practical considerations, to explain why they moved into Indische Buurt. For example, for local blogger Karlijn, the neighborhood "fits her ideals." Another told us they "feel at home" in Indische Buurt, while yet another referred to it as "my little neighborhood" (*mijn buurtje*). Several participants stated that they were "proud of the neighborhood." Anne, a young student who moved to Indische Buurt just a few months before meeting us for an interview, explained why she posted a picture of herself in her Oost sweatshirt in a bar in Javastraat. "I had just moved and it was my birthday. I had told everyone I moved to Oost and I was quite proud of that. I think that is why I posted the picture, telling people: yes, *I* am here now, too." She added that she wanted people to "see that I am having fun here, and that it's a nice neighborhood."

Residents underlined the uniqueness of Indische Buurt by comparing it to other neighborhoods in Amsterdam, like the tourism-dominated city center (Pinkster and Boterman 2017) or the suburban neighborhood of IJburg. For our research participants, being proud of living in the neighborhood and close to Javastraat was an important motivation for wanting to post about the neighborhood. They enjoyed following accounts that posted about restaurants, bars and stores in the neighborhood and sharing their own posts about visits to local establishments. Reading and posting about the neighborhood served to both valorize and enrich their presence in the neighborhood. They got more out of it that way.

Some of the Instagram users and bloggers appreciated the neighborhood not so much for what it was, but for what it was turning into. Some had friends and family who expressed concern about their move to a neighborhood still perceived as unsafe and peripheral. But the neighborhood's star was rising quickly. Derek, the meat enthusiast from earlier, was proud to be a part of the gentrification process. He explained that he was one of the first to recognize the street's "great potential."

> In a job interview at the municipality, I once said I would like to do something about Javastraat, because I thought it was such a nice street with great potential, but very little was happening there at the time. That job didn't work out, but that is how we came up with the idea for the blog. And now, seven and a half

> years later, I am kind of proud that I said that, seeing what has happened to the street now.

Several of our interlocutors likened their social media feeds to trophy cabinets. Christel, a lifestyle blogger, explained that she wanted to show she had been to "the new cool place." In her view, the neighborhood's status improved as hip places proliferated. "For young people, restaurants and bars are important and define the neighborhood." She was determined to show her followers how nice her neighborhood was. We asked if she herself was susceptible to such signals. With a laugh, she answered, "I try not be swayed easily by what I see online, but if I notice, like, alright, really everyone is going there—not to say that I would also immediately run to that place, but then I know it is apparently worth visiting, or it's just cool if you have been there."

Although many posts featured close-ups of hipster favorites, like cocktails and cupcakes, or rave reviews of upmarket boutiques and barber shops, some people we spoke to expressed ambivalence about the neighborhood's gentrification. Mare told us that the ethnic supermarkets, green grocers, and bakeries made her feel "like being on vacation." Several others told us they consider them convenient for buying cheap vegetables and special ingredients. We found a consensus among our research participants that Javastraat's multiculturalism contributes to its vibes and charm. And yet, such appreciation was not reflected in Instagram feeds or on local lifestyle blogs.

The vast majority of content we studied was produced by and for white, middle-class residents investing in Javastraat as a space of aspirational consumption. On rare occasions we came across social media users who identified with the street and the neighborhood for other reasons. For example, in a post tagging the popular brunch establishment Eastside, a young Black man wearing the Amsterdam-based streetwear brand Filling Pieces posed in front of his apartment door. Another post shows a close-up of another young Black man wearing a baseball cap with gothic letters spelling out Eastside (not related to the restaurant). The cap's typography was in clear contrast with the hipster aesthetics of the Oost shirts donned by other social media users. In an interview, the young man, a local rapper named Capa, explained why he wears the cap. "You just want to show where you're from, you know? 'This is me. This is what I stand for,' " he told us. "Look, rappers are the neighborhood and the city, you actually represent both. Wherever I go, when I wear that cap, they immediately know where I'm from."

While both Capa and gentrifiers wore place-branded clothing items, they did so for different reasons. The gentrifiers moved to the neighborhood because it matched their lifestyle aspirations. Signaling affinity was a way of valorizing the move and marking their newly found status. For Capa, in contrast, the Eastside cap reflects his rootedness in the neighborhood and thus told a very different story of local belonging.

Capa was an exception online but not in the neighborhood. Like him, young men and women residing in the neighborhood had been identifying with it long before it was "discovered" by gentrifiers. Sakızlıoğlu and Lees (2020), for example, discuss immigrant entrepreneurs who tell a very different story of the street. For them, the street was at its high point in the 1990s, when it provided ample opportunities to start businesses and attracted mostly immigrant consumers from the neighborhood and the urban region. Redevelopment and the emergence of new establishments was an imposition to which they had to adapt, whether they liked it or not.

Pushing for Gentrification

So far, we have discussed recurring patterns of uneven representation and the reasons why mainly new residents post and write about Oost and Javastraat. By and large, representations of place are aspirational products of new urbanites, not expressions of deep local roots. A further question concerns the material impact of such representations on the street itself. It is impossible to isolate the impact of representations, but it is possible to examine strategic orientation of such representations: what sorts of neighborhood change do they help to bring about?

Many of the posts resembled advertisements: they idealized consumption. Asked about her reasons for posting, Christel, who moved to Indische Buurt a few years earlier, told us that she wanted to express her pride in the neighborhood. As we found, that was a common motivation. But she had an additional motivation. "It also has to do with drawing attention to your neighborhood and supporting nice places," she told us. After a recent lunch at Eastside, she decided to post. "I really like the place and I think it should be seen . . . . People are more likely to go to places that are mentioned often."

By advertising places to their followers, social media users feel they can contribute to their success. We cannot know for sure whether these representations successfully attract copycat gentrifiers, but many posts are clearly meant to do just that. In marketing scholarship, this is known as "social proof" and is considered a priceless asset.

Sometimes posts *are* actual advertisements posted by the establishments' personnel, influencers, or marketing agencies. For instance, local blogger Karlijn built a network in the neighborhood through her online presence, and she often got invited for complimentary dinners or other treats in return for promoting places to her considerable following:

> I write about all the places I find cool, and I like encouraging people to go there too, also people from outside of Amsterdam. Sometimes these places invite me to come. For example, one restaurant always invites me whenever they have a new vegan menu for me to try. And I like to share that with others. This way it really becomes my neighborhood.

Another group displaying strong commitment to the neighborhood were the business owners of Javastraat. One of the new owners is Eline Bouman, who owned a new bar on Javastraat and lived close by. From the day it opened a few years ago, her bar has been incredibly popular among people from both inside and outside the neighborhood. It is one of the area's most frequently pictured places on Instagram and is often referred to as a "hot spot" in online reviews. In conversations with other entrepreneurs on the street, several refer to Eline's leading role as one of the first new entrepreneurs on Javastraat. In an interview, Eline explained how the local government's policy plan to stimulate the arrival of new cafés, bars, and restaurants on Javastraat (see Sakızlıoğlu and Lees 2020) convinced her to open her bar. She wanted to be the first to open a bar to appeal to the many "young, nice people" living in Indische Buurt:

> I don't want to sound arrogant, but things got started with my bar. The municipality had written that plan, but there was no one like me who really dared to do it this way. And so I was the first and I think that's special . . . . I have actually grown along with the neighborhood, as an entrepreneur and as a resident. Because the neighborhood has become more livable, and I have grown wiser in what I do. And the people that come here have embraced it all.

Later in the interview, Eline stated that "good" entrepreneurs like herself, who "pay taxes" and "care for the neighborhood," made Javastraat safer and brought economic growth.

The idea that "good" entrepreneurship can make a neighborhood safer and more livable is widely shared among other entrepreneurs and residents. In addition to Eline's bar, many mentioned the bars and restaurants of the Three Wise Men from the East, a team of three entrepreneurs who started one of the first bars in Oost targeting new middle-class residents in 2008. Ten years later, they owned ten different establishments in Oost and nine more in the rest of

Amsterdam, all of them Instagrammable to a fault. In November 2019, they were awarded Best Entrepreneurs of the Year by *entrée Magazine* for "reinventing the neighborhood bar" and "connecting to the neighborhood," as well as for their "innovative designs and concepts." Altogether, the new entrepreneurs' economic power and social reputation allows them to define the street and the direction it is taking, reinforcing the image of the street as an up-and-coming site of high-end consumption. The notion that Eline and the Three Wise Men are not just shrewd entrepreneurs but also a positive force for neighborhood change hinges on the idea that the street and the neighborhood previously had little that was worthy of appreciation or preservation.

This push for change also affects the aesthetics of the neighborhood as the streetscape is gradually brought in line with gentrifiers' aesthetic expectations (see Degen and Rose 2022). One example of how this new aesthetic took shape was an initiative by a graphic designer who lived in the neighborhood and wanted to celebrate that "Javastraat is the most colorful and surprising street of Amsterdam." He designed a set of a set of artistic postcards with Javastraat-centric slogans, such as "Cheers to the East."

Another example of aesthetic adaptation is an initiative by Aisha Tahiri, a creative entrepreneur, activist, and neighborhood resident with a Moroccan background. Aisha was a newcomer to the neighborhood—"I am a gentrifier too"—but she was very much concerned about the impact of gentrification. She argued that it was an outrage that the municipality heavily invested in the refurbishment of the street and the renewal of the neighborhood without considering that this might result in displacement. Although her analysis mostly focused on the capitalist logic underlying urban development, she suggested that aesthetic sensibilities and narratives also play an important role. Politicians, policy makers, and gentrifiers, she felt, often fail to recognize quality or value unless it is presented to them in an aesthetic register that they can understand. "These people have an Instagram vision," she told us, and this meant that the immigrant entrepreneurs fade into the background. When we asked her if she sees it as her task to educate new residents on what the neighborhood has to offer, she chuckled and smiled wryly, "If only. . . ." She wanted to change how gentrifiers perceive the neighborhood, but this was not within her power. So instead, she tried to change the environment according to the gentrifiers' "Instagram vision." She described her work as helping immigrant entrepreneurs make their shops "Insta-proof" by adapting their storefronts, signage, and offerings. She had some success—a couple of stores have been able to attract new customers in droves after their makeover—but she knew she could not thwart gentrification and displacement, only change its form.

Conclusion

Sharon Zukin (1995, ch. 1) describes the visual representation of the city as part of a battle over who owns the city. This battle is largely waged online today. Who goes into battle? Who emerges victorious? What are the spoils? The scholarship on subcultural fragmentation of social media users discussed in the previous chapters would lead us to expect there to be a multiplicity of geographically proximate but relationally separate subcultural groups. This is not what we find when zooming in on Javastraat. On the contrary, the representations of the street are strikingly coherent and uniformly push in one direction—that of gentrification. While scholarship in community and urban studies has long argued that the development of digital communication technology adds to, rather than supplants, local community relations and place belonging (Hampton 2016; Halegoua 2020), our analysis stresses the uneven nature of digital place-making. Yes, sense of place can be digitally enhanced, but this does not include everyone to the same degree.

The representations of Javastraat circulating online are not merely reflections. They shape how the street develops. They reflect and reinforce a changing balance of power between different groups within the city. People and money gravitate to places that stand out in the competition for attention. The posts of exalted consumption and conviviality picture the places in a positive light and are sometimes explicitly meant to draw in new people. While we cannot establish the independent impact of social media as they are woven into the fabric of everyday life, it is clear they work together with other forces in a hegemonic coalition promoting gentrification. The very same places that stand out on social media because they are tagged so often are routinely mentioned in city marketing brochures, Airbnb listings, local newspapers, and real estate advertisements. The mirror image of this process of celebration and amplification is that many other places—the working-class cafés, the community centers, the ethnic convenience stores, the hangouts of radical subcultures—drop in rank and become invisible. Instagram users conspire in a distributed production of indifference. The posts become part of the restructuring of the city in the image, and through the images, of gentrifiers.

7
Conclusion

Not long before taking on its new name of Meta in late 2021, Instagram's parent company was at the center of a series of revelations. The debates around these revelations provide a clear sense of the dominant narratives shaping public perception of social media. Initially called the Facebook Files in a series of reports by the *Wall Street Journal*, these disclosures became known as the Facebook Papers after whistleblower Frances Haugen came forward and testified before the United States Congress on October 5, 2021. In her testimony, Haugen stated that she believed the company's products "harm children, stoke division, and weaken our democracy." The revelations pertaining to Instagram packed a particular punch for youth advocates because the leaked documents revealed internal research suggesting that Instagram has a negative impact on the body image of young girls. "Facebook Knows Instagram Is Toxic for Teen Girls, Company Documents Show," read a headline in the *Wall Street Journal* on September 14 (Wells, Horwitz, and Seetharaman 2021). All this reporting and testifying added up to a full-blown moral panic, suggesting that social media are reshaping society in ways that harm individuals and undermine democracy.

The image of social media that informs these debates casts users as passive dupes and social media corporations as sophisticated manipulators. The Netflix documentary *The Social Dilemma* (Orlowski 2020), another key reference in public and scholarly debates during the time of our research, presented a similar picture, explicitly comparing social media to drugs. Dr. Anna Lembke, a professor of psychiatry, explains in *The Social Dilemma* that social media play on our basic biological imperative to connect with other

On Display. John D. Boy and Justus Uitermark, Oxford University Press. © Oxford University Press 2024.
DOI: 10.1093/oso/9780197629437.003.0007

people. What makes social media particularly insidious is that they are designed by the world's best engineers and powered by the most advanced computer systems. On the opposite end of our screens, explains former Google engineer turned tech critic, Tristan Harris, in the documentary, "there's these thousands of engineers and supercomputers that have goals that are different than your goals, and so, who's gonna win in that game?" A social media platform, Harris argues, is "seducing you. It's manipulating you. It wants things from you. And we've moved away from having a tools-based technology environment to an addiction and manipulation-based technology environment. That's what's changed. Social media isn't a tool that's just waiting to be used. It has its own goals, and it has its own means of pursuing them by using your psychology against you."

There are good reasons why the Facebook Papers and *The Social Dilemma* caused a stir—they provide a compelling narrative of how bright minds and sophisticated technologies are put to work to establish corporate domination over our digital spaces and, thereby, social life as a whole. There is no doubt that social media use generally, and Instagram use specifically, can have deleterious effects for some groups of users in some circumstances, and that these effects are important to understand.[1] However, when taking all available evidence into consideration, it is remarkable that the psychological effects of social media use are ambiguous and mixed. Sometimes it lifts people up, sometimes it puts them down; occasionally effects are to be found, more often they seem altogether absent (e.g., Valkenburg, Meier, and Beyens 2022).

Such complexity and ambivalence should caution us against ascribing responsibility for all sorts of social ills to social media. While there is reason to be critical of social media, it matters *how* we are critical. And it is here that we find dominant narratives of social media fall short—incidentally, much in the same way that dominant narratives of drugs fall short (Cohen 2000). They assign blame to specific substances (platforms or drugs) instead of considering the range of motivations people have for use and the broader sets of relations in which those substances achieve their effects. Taking this latter approach means that we do not seek to isolate the effect of social media, but rather consider how social media achieve their effects in conjunction with broader sets of relations and in the specific contexts in which they are embedded.

In this book we sought to develop such a contextual and relational approach. It is *contextual* because we believe that we can only understand what happens on a platform by studying the different types of environments in which it is embedded. Social media only play a role as a part of broader sets of relations; they're not a *deus ex machina*. Here "context" enters. For instance, we can only understand Instagram's role in reshaping the city by taking into consideration broader processes of urban change like gentrification or segregation. Our approach is *relational* because we believe that how individuals are composed—what they feel, want, or fear—is intimately related to how they are connected (de Swaan 2001; Emirbayer 1997; Elias 1978). Social media mediate relations and subjectivity, so we need to look at those in combination and examine people's invariably rich, fraught, and complex relationships with others and themselves.

Taking such a relational and contextual approach makes it difficult to arrive at a definitive verdict on social media in the way that *The Social Dilemma* and a slew of other popular jeremiads do. Instead, it allows us to see patterns and processes that we otherwise risk overlooking. In the remainder of this chapter, we recap the three main arguments of the book to spell out how our contextual and relational approach sheds light on dynamics which dominant narratives of social media are likely to miss. We then discuss how our arguments and findings relate to two academic projects which we see as closely aligned with our own: critical media studies, and computational social science.

Integration

First, we argue that Instagram is a force for *integration*. Scholars and commentators now often worry about the polarizing effects of social media, arguing that they sort us into distinct groups, reinforce beliefs through echo chambers and filters bubbles, and transform initially trivial variations of opinion into unshakable differences of identity (e.g., Törnberg et al. 2021). We do not deny that such mechanisms are operative, but our research suggests there are important countervailing tendencies as well, leading us to argue that social media often serve as vehicles of integration. Our computational analysis of Instagram networks in Amsterdam in Chapter 5 found that users cluster in different groups, but what stood out was that these groups were interconnected. These networks, we argue, do not separate people into different life-worlds but, in contrast, bring people into each other's purview, connecting them to each other in such a way that they cannot easily disregard what others think. The results of our computational analysis align with insights from our interviews, which suggest that Instagram users anticipate that their posts may be viewed by people who do not share their beliefs or preferences.

Throughout the previous chapters, we saw that heightened social integration has profound implications. They are full of accounts of how the performance of the self that users put on by way of their Instagram feeds is crafted with proximate *and* distant others in mind. Recall Lotte in Chapter 4, who told us about her worries of coming over as a killjoy. Even though she might prefer to interact mostly with other feminists, her online connections to her small-town neighbors resulted in her having to take their expectations into consideration when expressing herself. Other interviewees likewise censor their online expressions. Most obviously, they do not want to be seen smoking or eating pork chops. But they also do not, for instance, post pictures of their lovers unless they are in a stable relationship, share less than impressive professional achievements, or discuss doubts and uncertainties. With more and more diverse ties, users are bound in more and different ways, raising the odds that someone in their networks will not appreciate what they do or say. The effect of all these small instances of curation and censorship is that online personas are much more polished than actual messy persons.

This tension between the profile and the person results not in an acrimonious struggle *between* users, but occasions internal struggles *within* them. On the one hand, users enjoy creating online personas. There is joy in being able to hide what you're ashamed of and display what you're proud of. Creating online displays, moreover, is aspirational—it creates an idealized self to live up to and work toward. People develop in dialogue with others, with their profile functioning as an interface that they can playfully or strategically tweak. But on the other hand, the tension between the person and the profile is a cause of friction, even anxiety. Users feel alienated from their more successful online personas and still worry about not being sufficiently impressive. Moreover, the polished images of themselves that people put up become a mirror for others. Consuming an endless stream of beautiful, witty, and impressive images can be pleasurable, but it also induces a sense of failure and shortcoming. Social media are one important route through which others become internalized, transforming external constraint (Elias's *Fremdzwänge*) into internal ones (*Selbstzwänge*). The ritualized nature of self-display means that some users feel compelled to do it long after it has stopped paying off for them (Boy and Uitermark 2022).

Instagram-induced integration shapes not only subjectivities but also environments. In Chapter 5 we learned about the difficulty of sustaining a venerable safe space for Amsterdam's queer community when it becomes integrated into the general visual economy through the use of networked cameras, Instagram, and other social or review platforms. These transport the dominant gaze and stifle expressions considered deviant by remote onlookers. For some places, the only way to avoid this stifling gaze is to opt out of Instagram visibility altogether. Chapter 6, in turn, showed that some places and habitats thrive in the limelight of social media. As gentrifiers showcase consumption and express belonging they not only boost their own status, but also boost the visibility of the places they use as décor. The relentless aestheticization thus extends to urban landscapes and compels establishments of all sorts to conform to gentrifiers' tastes and standards. Regardless of whether it results in subtle or in overt sanctions, social integration makes it difficult to "make a scene," literally and figuratively. Subcultures need to embrace strategic forms of "balkanization" if they want to stand a chance.

While we qualify the argument that social media inexorably divide us, our discussion should make clear that we do not consider social integration to be an inherently good thing. Sociologists often stress the perils of polarization or emphasize the benefits of having wide-ranging social networks, which research shows can help in efforts to organize for collective action, gain information, or get support in times of hardship. However, social ties can also be conduits of a compulsion, foreclosing space for maneuver rather than expanding it (Berry and Sobieraj 2016; Sobieraj 2020; Marwick 2021). While such compulsion can take the form of harassment, in the everyday lives of most Instagram users it usually takes on more subtle forms. Generally speaking, users receive much more positive than negative feedback—they get only likes, not dislikes, and comments tend to be supportive (Valkenburg and Piotrowski 2017)—but they know that just because criticism is not overt does not mean it is not there. They realize that ruthless judgment is common, not in the least because they themselves judge harshly and gossip profusely. Being compelled to anticipate what others *might* think is a heavy social burden.

Many of our interviewees insist that the ultimate use of Instagram is to express yourself without consideration of what others might think—"you do you"; "haters gonna hate"; "only God can judge me"; and so on. Running through our interviews is a profound belief in the myth of the autonomous self—a self that must not compromised, and that should be expressed. But our interviewees also know, even if they do would like it to be otherwise, that the very purpose of posting is to come into the purview of others, which invariably means that these others become part of their selves.

Inequality

Second, Instagram thrives on *inequality*. Whereas in the 1990s and 2000s many observers considered lateral and horizontal relations a defining feature of digital technology, by now the *communis opinio* is that social media buttress long-standing inequalities, both among users and between users and corporations. Instagram is a shining example. The relations spun between Instagram users place them in highly stratified systems of rank. The platform is used by different groups for different purposes, but they all are assessed, whether they like it or not, through the same metrics: numbers of followers, likes, and viewers. Our computational analysis of networks of likes and comments found that the distributions of these field-specific valuations are highly uneven; they are not normally distributed but highly skewed (Boy and Uitermark 2017).

As a consequence, when people browse through timelines, they are not just looking; they are looking *up* or *down*. Viewing, as well as posting, is shot through with status differences, leading users to consider their position on the platform and, by extension, in society at large. The literature on social media and Instagram has examined this through the lens of *aspiration*. Remarkably, this was already the case in Alice Marwick's book *Status Update*, which analyzed tweets, blogs, and other parts of what was then called "web 2.0" as instances of "aspirational production" (Marwick 2013, 121–123). Work by Marwick and colleagues like Brooke Erin Duffy (2017) published since then further cements this emphasis through the concept of *aspirational labor*. What is it social media users aspire to? Existing scholarship mostly pays attention to how these aspirations shape the *productive* uses of social media rather than how it is consumed, and they mainly study those content creators who either have achieved significant Instafame or income or are pursuing it. One aim of this book is to round out the picture by studying users who are invested in Instagram but do not aspire to the status of influencer.

When studying these users, Chapter 3 argued, we must acknowledge that they look up most of the time. The people they follow are, on average, more accomplished, better looking, happier, and more energetic. While this is a general regularity in social networks that is known as the friendship paradox (Feld 1991), on Instagram it also results from a conscious decision of users to optimize their timelines for inspiration. People interested in lipstick or mascara follow accounts of make-up cognoscenti, aspiring football players follow professional footballers, budding artists follow established artists, and so on. This creates both anxiety and excitement—people are intimidated by the success of others, but they are also inspired and want to establish a reputation for themselves. Although our interviewees all, without exception, want to stay true to themselves, they also find themselves emulating those who are more successful. Users sense the social ranking that goes on, and even if they initially keep an ironic distance from the ideals their Instagram feeds present them with (as Sophie did when she picked up Instagram during her time in Bali), it is hard to avoid the aspirational draw to move up in the hierarchy. Central users with high follower counts provide the model for how to achieve this, with people lower in the hierarchy learning from them which poses, filters, clothes, and styles to use.

The motivation to achieve social standing is, in many cases, compounded by economic considerations: people want recognition on Instagram not just for its own sake, but also because this helps them get ahead professionally. Quite a few of our interviewees had discovered that an up-to-date and carefully curated profile helped them connect with prospective clients and employers. Others—theater actors, fashion designers, photographers, illustrators—indicated that being on Instagram was not just a way to get a leg up, but a vital means of survival in their respective fields. When Instagram becomes so important, simply quitting is not an option—it becomes imperative to organize your life, at least to some degree, around Instagram and the kind of aesthetic and aspirational labor it demands. The most central users—those with the most connections and the highest standing—often did not feel like they were in command at all, but had to work hard to keep up appearances, an imperative that was especially challenging when they were suffering in their personal lives or felt conflicted about which version of themselves they wanted to put online. Whereas Marwick and Duffy, as well as other scholars, including Crystal Abidin (2017), Betsy Wissinger (2015), and Sylvia Holla (2015), find that aspiring influencers, models, and professional cultural producers make enormous sacrifices in the pursuit of professional success, our findings suggest that even those who use Instagram on the side are captured by its *illusio*, pursuing its rewards and seeing the world through its aesthetics and metrics. Just as everything can potentially be commodified, everything can potentially be communicated, and therefore aestheticized, arranged, and curated to fit the picture. Instagram thus becomes second nature, adding a layer of complexity and creativity, but also imposing demands on situations and people, Are they Instagrammable? And, if not, can they be made to conform?

Instagram's aesthetic norms apply not just to people and experiences, but also to places. Just like some people used to put pins in a map of the world to mark where they had been, Instagram users can tag the places where they took pictures. The longer they use the app, the longer and more intense their investment, users come to see the city through and like Instagram, seeking out interesting details and contrasting colors but, above all, places that can serve as stages for status displays. Instagram constitutes a distinctive way of seeing that composes an image of the city that is sanitized and nearly devoid of negativity. Grit may be glamour, but otherwise the messiness and occasional gloom and doom of the city have no place in users' feeds. The urban imagination promoted by Instagram sees the city as a collection of "hot spots," and what is in between these hot spots gets the cold shoulder. The result of such selective representation is an extremely uneven distribution of visibility. Looking at the city as a whole, we found that fewer than two dozen Amsterdam locations account for one-fifth of all geotagged posts (Boy and Uitermark 2017). Zooming in on the street-level in Chapter 6, we found that nearly all the highly visible places on Javastraat were recently established stores and cafés catering to gentrifiers.

Digital inequality here does not take the form of unequal access, the traditional focus of research on digital inequality, but of unequal recognition and visibility. We found that white gentrifiers are much more likely than others to geotag their posts, laying a symbolic claim to the city and picturing it as their own. A cluster of predominantly white gentrifiers was six times as likely to geotag places as a cluster composed for the most part of young men and women of color (Boy and Uitermark 2017). As the natural experiment reported in Chapter 5 showed, the latter cluster disappeared from view altogether when geotags became opt-in. These dramatic differences suggest that some users are more disposed and better positioned to claim the city through Instagram than others, and that these differentials map onto other forms of social stratification. In Instagram's warped representation of Javastraat, highly visible locations are mostly trendy boutiques, bars, and cafés, while the older establishments, typically run by immigrants and catering to lower-income groups, disappear from view even though they still form the majority of the shops on the street. These results are significant on their own because aesthetics and visibility shape our imagination of what the city is, who belongs in it, and whom it belongs to

(Zukin 1995). But uneven representations online also have material effects on the ground. Instagram confirms the status and visibility of these geotagged places, further boosting their competitive position and their role as engines of gentrification. In this sense, Instagram not only feeds on but also reinscribes socio-spatial inequalities.

Conformity, Minute Deviations and Social Change

Third, Instagram engenders *conformity* and the staging of *minute deviations*. The pressure toward conformity is a result of integration into a stratified system of rank, as well as the mutual monitoring that social media in general, and Instagram in particular, enable. Recall our discussion of the court society in Chapter 2, which serves as a model to understand the cultural consequences of such a social situation. Within the court, individual courtiers tried to stand out, for instance, by adding to their plumage. However, such moves toward distinction were subject to structural pressures and had to be carefully calibrated. Instagram users similarly must reckon with structural pressures. They have some leeway in how to express themselves, and occasionally that allows them to use their accounts for political statements or, as in Nika's case in Chapter 4, cultivate a "counter-aesthetics." Most of the time, however, such protests or dissents are subtle.

Our study of Instagram feminism in Chapter 4 provides the best illustration of how this plays out in practice. We were interested to know what politics can look like in the mirage of representations that is Instagram. Some of our interviewees reported outright instances of self-censorship, while others experienced Instagram as an untrammeled opportunity to put their feminist politics on display. Most often, however, their experiences attest to what Yasmin described as an internal "war," wherein the desire for political expression clashes with the perceived promise of a successful

Instagram profile—and the peril of having it appear anything less than polished. Our interviewees made a variety of compromises to resolve this war, the combined effect of which was to engender minute deviations. One possibility for those who want to challenge dominant norms and still maintain visibility on Instagram is to do so by sneaking in a bit of messiness in an otherwise flawlessly composed image. Recall the images of Maya and Erika, who both resolved their respective struggles with compulsory visibility on Instagram by subtly tweaking the parameters of self-display. Another option is to assimilate feminism into the platform's reigning visual vernacular, so that it will not be perceived as jarring or unrelatable, but as an extension of one's brand. This was the path taken, with some frustration, by Sara, who found that a feminist identity was advantageous to her modeling career only for as long as it did not alienate powerful men. Finally, political expression may be transmuted from an explicit message into a subtle vibe, changing the emotional valence of an image without deviating from the overt norms of decorum.[2]

Although minute deviations tend to reinscribe the Instagram aesthetic, the resulting representations still aim to push for changes in what and who is considered worthy of visibility and recognition. Recognizing that Instagram visibility is a major avenue for the maintenance and accumulation of symbolic value (and that to lack it can amount to a form of abjection), critical Instagram users engage in the struggle over visibility using the only means available, which are themselves visual.

This struggle for visibility is waged for underrepresented people and for issues, and it also extends to places. As we showed in Chapter 6, owners of establishments lacking a strong online presence find themselves in a situation of having to "Insta-proof" their businesses if they want to maintain their offline presence in gentrifying neighborhoods. They do so by redesigning storefronts, posting appealing images, and rebranding traditional foodstuffs like chai and bulgur as "superfoods." Through actions like this, the city is gradually restructured in the image, and through the images, of gentrifiers. At the same time, places that before were invisible become part of how the city is imagined on Instagram, even if not on their own terms.

Aisha, who advised several of the businesses on Javastraat, told us that she felt there was no way to change people's perceptions—racialized images of what constitutes an appealing or interesting place are too deeply ingrained—but also that Two Rivers Deli, a store operated by Syrians, *won* (her emphasis) when they successfully restyled their nondescript store and turned it into an appealing delicatessen that consistently attracts a queue of patrons during lunch and dinner times. Similarly, Luna would like the Vondel Gym's Instagram presence to direct positive attention to members of groups who are otherwise shunned in the fitness world, but it can do so only on the margins.

We showed that people are conflicted about politics and choose subtle expressions over outspoken statements. These findings can be read in different ways. One might argue that Instagram is antithetical to politics and demands aesthetic conformity, which is true. Such conformity is consequential because it elevates some messages and messengers over others, precluding, or at least discouraging, people who do not meet beauty norms or have a firm grasp on the platform vernacular. One could also make the case that all these subtle expressions together result in slow yet seismic shifts, gradually changing what is considered beautiful, trendy, or worthwhile. The pressure to conform and the desire to impress do not pre-empt calls for change, but they render them subtle and minute. This type of politics is certainly less forceful, but it is also more widespread and therefore possibly more consequential.

Whether such politics are essentially conformist or potentially revolutionary is not a question we can answer conclusively. Regardless, what we see here is very different from how social media's role in social change is usually conceived. Whereas many researchers have focused on how tight-knit groups of committed activists use social media to organize outside the state and the cultural mainstream (e.g., Manuel Castells and many following his lead), our research calls attention to the mundane politics of Instagram—the occasional post, the subtle gesture.

Instagram's Affordances and Neoliberal Sensibilities

When Alice Marwick wrote in 2013 that social media serve as extensions of market relations into everyday life, her main point of reference was Twitter. As we finalize this book a decade later, it is Instagram that comes to mind as a picture-book illustration of Marwick's claim. Instagram is where people present themselves as ideal subjects of neoliberal society. They showcase their accomplishments and consume profusely; they rarely complain and, when they do, it is usually not about poor working conditions or inequality. Seen in this light, the "influencer," a figure birthed by Instagram, epitomizes total commodification, relentlessly competing for attention, turning their personalities into brands, and promoting just about anything if the money is right (and even if they do not get paid see Duffy 2017). Going over the profiles of influencers one might get the impression that Instagram is *designed* to commodify personhood and that influencers most readily play the role the platform's users are scripted to perform.

This characterization of Instagram, however, is not the whole story. There is another side to Instagram, and it has been there from the start. *No Filter* (2020), Sarah Frier's history of the platform, suggests that the founders, Kevin Systrom and Mike Krieger, conceived Instagram as a site for artistic creativity and spontaneous expression. In the early days of Instagram, they envisioned Instagram as a tool for capturing moments and turning them into memories. When recruiting the first users for the app, they sought out photographers and cultural producers who had the ability to spot beauty in the seemingly mundane or trivial. Instagrammers, at that point, formed artistic communities that together found new ways of registering their environments, elevating everyday streetscapes into art—everything from bricks to trees could be captured and transformed into a tile-shaped digital artwork. That Instagram came to be so widely used for purposes of self-promotion was unexpected:

> As the founders discovered that growing numbers of people, including the celebrities they had themselves sought out to promote the app, were using Instagram to showcase their status and promote their work, they were dismayed. In 2014, when Instagram had around 300 million users, they admonished those who abused the platform for reputational or material gain. The Instagram User Guide stated, "When you engage in self-promotional behavior of any kind on Instagram, it makes people who have shared that moment with you feel sad inside . . . . we ask that you keep your interactions on Instagram meaningful and genuine." (Frier 2020, 155)

The authenticity and creativity that the founders and early users valued so highly[3] has not disappeared. It might not be the first thing that comes to mind when you ask people about Instagram, but the creation and curation of posts is often done with care and creativity. Browsing through Instagram feeds will still provide you with an intimate sense of what people value as they artfully craft visual mementos of the people they hold dear and the moments they value. While it is certainly true that gentrified establishments are disproportionally pictured on Instagram, the places that are most often geotagged are public parks. A brood of ducklings or a picnic with friends can be just as Instagrammable as exquisite cocktails or impeccable latte art.

What this suggests is that the sort of aspirational displays that Instagram has become known for are not simply a function of its affordances. The visuality of Instagram posts, the possibilities to manipulate images through filters and editing, and the like buttons all help to turn the platform into a stratified system of rank in which users and their posts are continuously appraised, but this, in itself, does not explain ostentatious self-promotion. To account for this, we should not only look at the platform, but also at the *contexts* in which it is used and the *relations* in which it is embedded. For many of our interviewees in cultural industries like fashion, design, modeling, and marketing, self-promotion is not an act of personal vanity meant to make others "feel sad inside"; it is a necessary survival strategy in competitive environments where precarity is endemic and reputation paramount.

Doing well on Instagram is rewarding not just in terms of the platform's own elusive *illusio*, but it contributes to success in other fields. Just as Instagram facilitates rather than originates self-promotion, it also reinforces rather than imposes the collapse of private and public spheres. Users relying on the platform for self-promotion are enticed to strategically disclose their personal lives in an effort to put themselves on the market. As they put themselves on display for the market, the market in turn reaches deep into their lives, turning every aspect into something that might be valorized for reputational gain, which in turn might be valorized for social advancement and material rewards. Neoliberal sensibilities are nurtured when it becomes second nature to think of social life as a series of moments with the potential of furthering one's pursuit of status. Instagram brings the market close: it's always there, at your fingertips, it shapes how you view the world, and it tells you where you stand. It is not that Instagram is the origin of neoliberal sensibilities and relations, but it accommodates and reinforces them by making them more visible and visceral.

If Instagram's affordances are important but do not act on their own, this means that changing Instagram's functionalities will make a difference, but not a big one. The introduction of the Stories feature allowed users to post a series of pictures that automatically disappear after a day, and the optional removal of the likes counter served to increased engagement and accommodate a broader range of practices and expressions. These design changes, however, do not change the contradiction inherent in Instagram: messages will always take on a dual form as expressions of the self *and* strategic displays in a market of attention and appraisal. This duality makes posting, as well as viewing, such a contradictory, ambivalent experience. When psychologists find that Instagram does not have straightforward effects, this is not because it does not matter much, but because the platform incorporates the contradictions and tensions of the social worlds in which it is used.

Situated Computational Social Science

The proliferation of digital platforms has not only changed social life itself, but also the way it is studied. One powerful new strand of research sees the proliferation of digital data and the development of new computational methods as an opportunity to bring the social sciences up to speed with the natural sciences. The sociologist Duncan Watts argued over a decade ago that the "rapidly increasing availability of observational data, along with the ability to conduct experiments on a previously unimaginable scale, is allowing social scientists to imagine a world where at least some forms of collective human behavior can be measured and understood, possibly even predicted, in the way in which scientists in other fields have long been accustomed" (Watts 2011, 261). Since Watts's prognosis, a veritable interdisciplinary field, computational social science, has developed to deliver on the promises of digitization. While this field is epistemologically diverse, much of the research uses modeling, experiments, and statistical inference to identify patterns and mechanisms (Törnberg and Uitermark 2021). As computational social science searches for regularities across contexts and attempts to isolate mechanisms through experimental research, meaning and context are given short shrift or ignored altogether.[4]

Our research, in contrast, is based on the conviction that understanding the origins and effects of social media require us to *situate* them in the contexts in which they are used, and to examine the meaning conveyed through digital communication (Uitermark and van Meeteren 2021). To better understand digital platforms, we—paradoxically—need to de-center them and study the mutual constitution between digital platforms and the diverse contexts in which they are used (see Miller et al. 2016). For example, Chapter 5 not only examines the topology of Instagram networks but also examines how such networks are grounded in places within the city. We found that the people and organizations operating accounts that garner a lot of attention use their prominence to strategically shape how places are used, attempting to draw in or keep out certain groups and promoting particular values. In contrast to what we expected, the museums, gyms, and clubs at the very center of the network do not necessarily maximize engagement but instead attempt use their prominence to—usually slightly—challenge mainstream assumptions of what good art, bodies, and parties look like. Through this kind of research, we can move beyond media-centrism (Couldry 2012) and digital dualism (Maddox 2017), examining not just the contents and patterns of digital communication, but their origins and effects.

While our contextual and relational approach is primed to see contingency and ambiguity, it also enables us to see processes operating across different levels that, in much of social science analysis, are studied separately (Bourdieu 1990). By focusing on a particular city and a particular platform, we could observe how the digital connections fostered by Instagram serve as a conduit for extending and deepening competition. The compulsion for competition permeates relations, places, and people, contributing to neoliberal formations and subjectivities. Competition for status is pervasive and enters the minutiae of everyday life, even if most of our interviewees insist that the drive to compete undermines the authenticity that they so much value.

While our situated computational analysis offers advantages, we should acknowledge that there are trade-offs. The stipulation that research must be situated means that it is of necessity rather specific, even parochial—we cannot generalize from Instagram to all social media platforms, from our specific sample of active users to all users, or from Amsterdam to all cities. For instance, by grounding our study in Amsterdam, we have chosen a location that is known for resisting disintegration and inequality (Uitermark 2009). Our results may have looked different had we focused on a more divided city. Similarly, we feel that neoliberal society is an apt concept to capture the confluence of growing labor market precarity, widening inequality, privatization in Amsterdam, and the competition endemic to Instagram, but it might not be the most useful concept in other places or for other platforms.

Considering these specificities, we concede that our findings do not seamlessly generalize to other populations or platforms. But the same is true for other research based on data sourced from, say, Twitter or Facebook, that informs competing diagnoses about social media in contemporary society. One way to account for the differences between our observations of Instagram and others' observations of Twitter and Facebook is to trace them back to the affordances of different platforms (see van Dijck 2013; Bucher and Helmond 2017). On this reading, the patterns of interconnection and pressures toward conformity we observe are peculiar to Instagram and the specific possibilities for action the application offers its users. Although we readily agree that platforms provide different sets of features, we feel this kind of argument is limited by its privileging of the technological underpinnings of social relations.

Theorizing about affordances originated from the need to move beyond technological determinism and explicitly acknowledge that the same technological set-up allows for different kinds of social relations to emerge (Wellman et al. 2003). And yet, technology very often remains the starting and end point of analysis—whatever happens, happens because technology affords it, leading researchers to scrutinize design decisions in minute detail instead of considering the broader sets of relations and contexts in which digital technologies are used. A recent corrective to the analysis of affordances by Jenny L. Davis (2020) seeks to direct discussions away from *what* technologies afford to *how* they afford. The hope, Davis states, is that such an analysis will encompass more of the contextual variability in how systems affect human behavior. Affordances matter, but broader conditions matter as well.

Our proposal is that these broader contextual conditions may be more important than the particulars of different technologies. In the case of social media, there are certainly important variations between platforms, but it is nevertheless possible to discern common trends. While the internet initially functioned and felt like an alternate reality, it became increasingly woven into everyday life.[5] Social media accounts make the internet more personalized, intimate, and visual, while also making interdependencies more extensive, differentiated, and dense. The relational patterns we identify here emerge within this structural context: as we construct our personas and connections through social media, we are compelled to consider the views of proximate and distant others. The processes and mechanisms we identify on Instagram may be less salient on other platforms, but we surmise they *are* present there, too.

So, what is the use of our case? We would suggest that Instagram provides an alternative starting point for theorizing.[6] Where researchers of political communication on Twitter or Facebook use their specific cases to theorize about polarization, we can use our study of Instagram to highlight mechanisms of integration. Where researchers of political communication view social media posts as expressions of opinion, our case pushes us to consider them as status displays. Our theoretical perspective applied to a specific set of data enables us to identify processes and dimensions that may not have caught the attention of researchers working from a different theoretical perspective and studying different platforms. This understanding of how particular cases contribute to general theorization provides a rationale for future research. Just as we have brought theoretical and empirical work by others into conversation with our cases, we hope that others will do the same and extend, or qualify, the arguments developed in this book, multiplying the sites of research to identify a broader range of patterns and processes.

Tick-Tock

As we finish this book, TikTok is gradually relegating Instagram to the status which it, in turn, bestowed on Facebook for an earlier generation of younger users: the platform that your parents use. While its star is not yet fading, Instagram's cultural significance is transforming—not least because its parent company now has its eyes set on an as-yet undefined "metaverse." Given all this, it is fair to ask, why do we still bother publishing a book in today's fast-moving media environment? Tick-tock, indeed.

The answer is that, even though this is a book about Instagram, we hope that it contains lessons that will outlive any particular social media platform or fad. Whatever is next for humankind's large-scale experiment with social media, we are convinced that making sense of it, critiquing it, and telling a nuanced story about it will require us to look contextually and relationally. That takes time and careful analysis, otherwise we end up simply retreading dominant storylines. Integration, inequality, and conformity may remain central themes in future narratives, or they may be superseded by a new set of concerns—a new default setting. In any case, no silver bullet—be they design changes, such as removing metrics; government regulations mandating stricter content moderation;

or changes to the ownership structure of major platforms—will "solve" the issues with social media. A contextual and relational understanding will help us understand the trade-offs of various proposals and ensure that debates do not become encased in unhelpful myths.

APPENDIX

A Note on Methods

Our ambition to take a relational and contextual approach to Instagram meant that we worked with a mix of methods over the course of our research. This mix included both computational and qualitative methods as we sought to investigate both the broader structure of social relations on Instagram and the evolving sensibilities of Instagram users. While such a methods mix has become more common (e.g., Nelson 2017; Pardo-Guerra and Pahwa 2022), when we first started our project, we did not yet know of any examples to guide us. In the beginning phase, our research design evolved through a process of trial and error, but we quickly settled into a way of working that took us from computational analyses into the field and back again, honing questions and insights as we went along.

In what follows, we first describe how we collected and used platform data in our work. Next, we discuss the methods we used chapter by chapter, as some chapters were originally relatively independent subprojects carried out with different collaborators and varying research questions.[1] This means that we recruited Instagram users to talk to over the years (often vicariously through research assistants) in different ways.

Working with Platform Data

Until June 2016, Instagram allowed nearly unfettered access to posts and a wide range of associated metadata via its application programming interface (API). Using this interface and a custom-made tool (Boy 2015), we were able download all posts and metadata to which users had attached geotags or geocoordinates locating them in Amsterdam (as well as Copenhagen and a few smaller cities) for six months. We also collected all interactions (likes and comments) on posts within the first twenty-four hours.

The total volume of data collected in this way was very large. In line with our research interests, we confined our analysis to posts by longer-term residents, eliminating one-off posts or posts by users who were active for only a short period, to eliminate likely tourists. We also made the choice to focus on our data from Amsterdam almost exclusively, making only limited use of the data collected from the Danish capital for Chapter 4, and none from the smaller cities. The resulting Amsterdam dataset contained 709,348 posts by 78,207 users and

34.4 million interactions. Of those interactions, 130,665 were reciprocated between local users.

Recognizing the sensitive nature of this data, we observed a strict protocol. We restricted access to the PostgreSQL database holding the platform data and only reported on it in aggregate, taking care not to reveal personally identifiable information on any users. We performed computational analyses in a reproducible way using Jupyter Notebooks (Kluyver et al. 2016), drawing on the strengths of the scientific Python ecosystem. Two techniques were especially important as we worked with this data.

First, using *geographic analysis*, for which we leveraged several Python packages for geographic data science (Gillies 2013; Whitaker 2016), we analyzed spatial patterns in the distribution of posts, paying special attention to emerging "hot spots" where Instagram activity was concentrated. We constructed cluster maps as well as dynamic heat maps, which we inspected at various scales to understand which areas and establishments were attracting the most activity and how such patterns were changing over time.

Second, using *network analysis*, supported by the igraph network analysis package and its Python bindings (Csardi and Nepusz 2006), we constructed directed and undirected graphs based on the interactions between Instagram users in our data. We used centrality analysis, and especially the PageRank algorithm, to identify influential users, many of whom we contacted as potential interviewees. Community detection allowed us to identify clusters of users bound together by stronger and denser reciprocated ties.[2] To characterize these clusters, we used a combination of automated and manual techniques. We used text analysis to find characteristic keywords in user bios per cluster (as indicated by a high *tf-idf* score). This often provided strong hints that members of a cluster had certain shared interests in, for example, specialty coffee or electronic dance music. We further performed a manual inspection of the ten most central accounts in each subgraph, looking for commonalities among them. For instance, when we found references to "personal body plans" in bios and spotted pictures of people flexing their muscles in gyms, we chose the label of "Fitness Enthusiasts" for a cluster.

After Instagram restricted access to its API, we decided not to resort to other ways of obtaining platform data, such as web scraping (Freelon 2018). Instead, we worked with what we had and shifted our emphasis to field research. As our interest was to study broad patterns in social relations, and not to keep up with the vacillations of the platform, we felt this was a better use of our time.

Contextualizing a Platform

For Chapter 3, we first interviewed six university students to pretest our interview protocol. We then used centrality analysis to select prominent users.

We divided our Amsterdam data into twenty-two official administrative areas (*gebieden*) and ranked users according to their centrality in the network formed by mutual likes and comments in each area as well as in the city as a whole (see Boy and Uitermark 2017). We reached out to the individuals so identified, resulting in eight interviews with prominent users. We did seven of these interviews in 2015 and one in 2020. The interview with a prominent user from 2020 was with someone who had indicated in 2015 that he wanted to participate but did not have the time. Because the fall-out of COVID-19 meant his gigs as a deejay were canceled, he had the time to talk to us in 2020.

We soon discovered that these central figures were not "influencers" in the conventional sense that they made a living by advertising products on their social media channels, but rather they were people working at the intersection of different scenes, like fashion, marketing, fitness, or art. They did have many followers—ranging from eight hundred to fifty thousand—but not nearly as many as professional influencers have. We suspect that the PageRank algorithm ranked them as most central because they posted frequently and because people engaging with their posts also had above-average centrality within the urban-scale network.

After Instagram shuttered its API, we adopted different methods to recruit interviewees. Snowball sampling was one. We asked the interviewees we recruited for Chapter 4, as well as Instagram users in our own social circles, whether they knew people that would be interesting for us to talk to. We explained to those interviewees that we wanted to have a sample of frequent Instagram users that was diverse in terms of gender, sexual orientation, and profession or education. We further specified that we liked to talk to people who liked to talk to us. As the interviews dealt with sensitive topics like self-image, aspirations, and social relations, interviewees needed to be prepared to open up and give a significant amount of time. This resulted in a further thirteen interviews, conducted mainly by Marije Peute in 2019 and 2020. We also re-interviewed two people we had talked to in 2015 to get a sense of how their lives and Instagram use had changed over the course of five years.

The interviewees in this second round had between 340 and twenty-seven thousand followers at the time of the interview. A handful of interviewees regularly received merchandise to promote on their channels or invitations to openings and events. Two regularly received substantial compensation for sponsored posts, but none of the interviewees relied on Instagram as their chief source of income. The full sample used in Chapter 3 thus comprises twenty-one interviews with frequent and central users.

We used both predefined and inductively derived codes to analyze the twenty-one interviews. The predefined codes had to do with the Eliasian theme of the interconnections between emotions like anxiety, excitement, and shame and the structure of social relations as mediated through Instagram. Inductively derived codes were used to cover themes that emerged in the interviews, including, for instance, the sharp differences with respect to the moods people had when they were posting and viewing, respectively. To allow space for individual stories in this chapter, we mention only ten interviewees by name (pseudonym) and cite examples from their interviews. Their stories cover the themes we found to be most relevant in our analysis of our interview material.

For Chapter 4, we found the first twelve of our total of twenty-five interviewees by querying data gathered from Amsterdam and Copenhagen via the erstwhile API, as described above. We searched for users who used the word "feminist" or "feminism" either in their user profile or in post captions, which include hashtags. This initial sampling frame thus included everyday users of the platform who affiliated with feminism through the platform's affordances. As such, they had made an explicit connection between Instagram and feminism, minimally signaling their interest in feminism on the platform, maximally using it as a device in their activism. We then recruited thirteen additional interviewees via snowball sampling (i.e., having interviewees recommend additional people to talk to). In this way, we broadened the range of interviewees beyond the initial population of north-western European urbanites, while also including more widely known users whose feminist affiliation is more broadly recognized.

Laura Savolainen conducted twenty-four of the interviews, Justus Uitermark conducted one. The interviews lasted for about an hour. Savolainen first worked on this project as an intern working under the supervision of Justus Uitermark, with John Boy providing technical assistance and advice; later, she continued her work on Instagram feminism as a thesis student, again under the supervision of Justus Uitermark. The three of us agreed early in the process that this research would result in a chapter in this book and a separate journal article with Savolainen as main author.

The interview questions explored our interviewees' Instagram use and their views on feminism before discussing how the two did, or did not, come together. We did not impose our own normative understandings of feminism but instead let our respondents explain what sort of practices or ideas they regarded as feminist. We transcribed interviews and coded them, identifying patterned and recurring contradictions and inner struggles interviewees reported feeling when using Instagram. In this inductive way, we discovered the filtering practices by which users attempt to reconcile their dissonant aims in using the platform. As our analysis shows, taken together, these filtering practices shape the feminist politics, imaginaries, and subjectivities that are cultivated on and communicated through Instagram.

The analysis in Chapter 5 was initially based entirely on platform data. With combined techniques from geographic and network analysis described above, we put to the test a number of hypotheses about social media's impact on enclave formation in cities. As we thought more about the tensions that emerge at the interface between Instagram and the city following some informal interviews with restaurant owners and employees in the cultural sector, we increasingly found it important to refine our insights in conversation with first-hand accounts of how places manage their online presence. From 2018 to 2020, Marije Peute conducted semi-structured interviews with seven marketing professionals, public relations consultants, and entrepreneurs. We recruited interviewees by contacting places tagged by Instagram users, taking care to cover each of the "zones" we identified with at least one interview. In addition, Peute visited several clubs and specialty coffee bars around Amsterdam, writing fieldnotes about her observations that focused on how these places invite or evade social media visibility. These qualitative insights served to further refine our understanding of social integration through Instagram and the tensions to which it gives rise.

Chapter 6 reports on research centered on a single street, the Javastraat, in Amsterdam's Indische Buurt ("Indonesian Quarter"). It builds on thirteen in-depth interviews conducted on location with residents, entrepreneurs, and artists who were prominent online. Irene Bronsvoort conducted twelve of these interviews, which lasted between one and two hours, as part of her research for a master's thesis, advised by Justus Uitermark, in 2016. Questions focused on residents' and entrepreneurs' attitudes toward their street, as well as their interests and motivations for posting about it. Justus Uitermark did an additional on-site interview with the entrepreneur we call Aisha Tahiri in 2020.

In addition to these interviews, we again drew on the Instagram data we had previously collected. Selecting posts with geocoordinates on or adjacent to the Javastraat, we obtained a dataset of 748 posts. This included posts that were not specifically about the street, so we selected the posts that referred to the street by name or tagged a location on the street. This smaller sample of ninety-eight posts served as a way to understand the range of representations circulating about the street on Instagram and the kinds of users creating these posts.

Notes

Chapter 1

1. This was the Cultural Conflict 2.0 project, funded by the Research Council of Norway and led by Professor David Herbert. After the completion of this project, we continued research for the book as part of ODYCCEUS, an EU-funded project that brought together natural and social scientists to study online conflict. Both projects, and so many like them, worked on the assumption that social media create echo chambers and amplify political conflict. As we explain below, we now suggest that a different point of departure is more fruitful.
2. We are not alone in proposing a "return to Elias" in this context. Media scholars Nick Couldry and Andreas Hepp draw extensively on Elias's concept of "figurations" in *The Mediated Construction of Reality* (2018). This concept allows them to capture emergent complexities in the media system while remaining attuned to the continued importance of human meaning-making. See also Couldry (2022) and Herbert and Fisher-Høyrem (2022).
3. In our understanding, neoliberal society is defined by social relations that mirror market relations, a norm of generalized competition, and—most importantly—the understanding that individuals should think and act as if they were an enterprise (see Dardot and Laval 2017).
4. At the time of writing, January 2023, the reference database Dimensions contained over fifty-eight thousand articles with "Twitter" in the title or abstract, and over fifty-six thousand articles with "Facebook," versus only twenty thousand for "Instagram." We believe these numbers, although stark, actually *underestimate* the profound impact of Twitter on how scholars imagine social media. Twitter is where polarization, protest, and misinformation—today's predominant scholarly concerns about social media—could be readily observed and researched. Anecdotally, many academics spend far more time on Twitter than on Facebook or Instagram.

Chapter 2

1. We are not alone in our exasperation. As early as 2002, the political philosopher Jodi Dean roundly rejected the public sphere prism on the grounds that the internet's underlying technological infrastructure has been designed to facilitate the pervasive commodification of social relations (Dean 2002, 2003). Alice Marwick (2013) views the philosophy and design of social media as an expression of the Californian Ideology which, while rooted in the libertarian culture of Silicon Valley, poses as universal. Terri Senft's essay "Hating Habermas" (nothing personal, she assures us) tells the story of how she came to feel increasingly convinced that the category of the public sphere did not help to make sense of the anger, bullying, and shaming that besieged her online (Senft 2020). We can even add Habermas himself to the list. One of the core arguments in *The Structural Transformation of the Public Sphere* is that tendencies toward the public sphere's collapse are "unmistakable, for while its scope is expanding impressively, its function has become progressively insignificant" (Habermas 1991, 4). More recently, he argued that there has been "incredible expansion of media publicity and an unprecedented densification of communication networks" while simultaneously "informalization and dedifferentiation" have eroded the public sphere (Habermas 2006, 556; our translation).
2. We use the somewhat broader moniker of relational sociology rather than Elias's preferred term, process sociology, to indicate that we also incorporate other theoretical influences.
3. Although *The Structural Transformation of the Public Sphere* has been read mostly as an attempt to formulate a normative model of the public sphere, it contains a sophisticated analysis of the symbolic economy of the court that is very much in line with Elias. For instance, Habermas also calls attention to "the stress of the grand festivities; these served not so much the pleasure of the participants as the demonstration of grandeur, that is, the grandeur of the hosts and guests" (Habermas 1991, 10).
4. Habermas also recognized that the public–private division is peculiar to the bourgeois public sphere. Like Elias, he extensively discusses the layout of houses and palaces to gauge the architectural inscription of the division or the lack thereof: "[B]eginning with Versailles, the royal bedroom develops into the palace's second center. If one finds here the bed set up like a stage, placed on a platform, a throne for lying down, separated by a barrier from the area for the spectator, this is so because in fact this room is the scene of the daily ceremonies of *lever* and *coucher*, where what is most

intimate is raised to public importance" (Richard Alewyn, as quoted in Habermas 1991, 10).

5. The concept of reflexivity will return in the following chapters. A brief definition seems in order, especially because the concept signifies the opposite of what everyday uses of the word may suggest. To act reflexively means not to act out of *reflex* (i.e., automatically), but after *reflecting* on oneself, one's actions, and one's thought process on a meta level (i.e., deliberately). Sociologists use a variety of metaphors to understand this process of taking oneself as an object of deliberation, such as looking at oneself in the mirror (Cooley 1956), having an internal conversation (Archer 2007), and breaking with one's habitual or spontaneous ways (Bourdieu 2000). Social change, uncertainty, and risk render such processes more salient in late-modern biographies (Beck, Giddens, and Lash 1994).
6. Her story is also discussed by Duffy (2017).
7. Further to this paradox, consider that Instagram users who set up an alternate account with more candid images of themselves refer to this "more real" alternate as their "fake Instagram," or "finsta."
8. The anthropologist Crystal Abidin (2016a) reports being asked by an academic following a conference presentation, "Aren't these just young, rich women doing vain things online?"

Chapter 4

1. This chapter is based on Savolainen, Uitermark, and Boy (2022).

Chapter 5

1. The anthropologist Jessa Lingel has written about several groups that used to make a home on the open web during the 1990s, only to be gradually displaced by the ascendant social media platforms in the 2000s. One of her studies focuses on extreme body modification, a subculture that for many years had a virtual meeting place at Body Modification Ezine (BME). The founders of BME positioned the platform as an "online haven for outsiders" (Lingel 2017, 37) where members could share their experiences with face tattoos, scarification, subincisions, stretched ears, piercings, flesh pulls, split tongues, and the like. The site flourished in the late 1990s but faltered as Facebook rose to prominence. The promise of a wider audience pulled members away from BME and onto social media like Facebook where

body modifiers' sense of alterity and community dwindled. Writer Liz Pelly (2019) details how do-it-yourself (DIY) cultural spaces from California to the United Kingdom started relying on Facebook and Instagram to promote events, which came to undermine their "scrappy" ethos.

2. Place tags are often rather generic. For instance, users could tag their picture with "Amsterdam" or "Amsterdam West." For the analysis that follows, we restricted our analysis to clearly defined places on the assumption that they convey a status signal when they are tagged. We eliminated places with a lot of variation in the rooftop coordinates associated with them. This includes place tags for large parks, long streets, or entire neighborhoods. We manually verified the remaining places, keeping 51.2 percent of tagged locations. There are 1,750 places in Amsterdam that people across clusters tag. Using this list, we look at the co-occurrence of places among users across clusters.
3. In addition to the nine largest clusters shown in Table 5.1, we identify several smaller ones. They include, in order of decreasing size, international students (1,120 users), Amsterdammers of Turkish descent (821), coffee aficionados (769), Russian-speaking expats (519), Evangelicals (395), CrossFit adherents (350), and Electronic Dance Music enthusiasts (304).
4. In line with the perspective outlined in Chapter 2, we do not interpret place tags as "trace data" that can be used to track users' trajectories through the city, but as features of status displays. Users typically do not post about their daily errands or their commute to work, but selectively and strategically use Instagram as a platform to live out their identities and showcase their social contacts, sense of style, achievements, or new purchases (see Hochman and Manovich 2013; Zasina 2018).
5. We were able to gather Yelp data for just over one-half of the places in our database.
6. The average Yelp rating of 4.15 is noticeably higher than the overall average (4.0), indicating that places in this zone are viewed favorably not just by the Instagrammers who tag them, but by Yelp reviewers as well. Second, Yelp indicates how costly establishments are through the use of repeated dollar signs ($, $$, $$$, and $$$$). Again, the lifestyle establishments score highest, with an average of 2.4 dollar signs, compared to an overall average of just 2.28. In both cases the differences are slight but significant and further support the impression that the lifestyle zone comprises high-status establishments. We performed a *t*-test of statistical significance ($p < 0.01$).
7. In the fitness territory, 3.4 percent of post captions (which include hashtags) contain "selfie," as opposed to 0.9 percent overall.

8. Individual social media users know this all too well and often respond by keeping their different social circles apart online (Costa 2018). For places like restaurants or clubs, though, there is no way they can do this, which means their proprietors must find different ways to reckon with multiple audiences and diverging expectations.
9. One way to achieve this kind of closure is to "deplatform" and migrate to messaging platforms (Rogers 2020). That comes at a high cost, though, which is why many "countercultural" folks want to stay on the mainstream platforms. Whatever these communities choose to do, it's clear that Instagram has changed the politics of visibility for them. Even De Trut is now on Instagram; however, they only post announcements and not photos.

Chapter 6

1. This chapter is based on Bronsvoort and Uitermark (2022).
2. See Zukin, Lindeman, and Hurson (2017), who coined this term to analyze the activities of New Yorkers writing Yelp reviews.

Chapter 7

1. As Gillespie (2018) shows, the politics of content moderation on social media platforms—a central flashpoint in the regulation of big tech—is closely tied to the psychological risks ascribed to social media.
2. Related to this, Papacharissi (2014) has argued that digital networks derive their power from the opportunities for emotional attunement that they provide. We get to feel part of something bigger, get excited about events halfway around the globe, or feel the outrage others laboriously put on display.
3. The founders had a genuine appreciation for authenticity and creativity (see also Thornton 2016), but there is also an important business case for protecting these values. Any kind of promotion, including self-promotion, can draw people away from the app. (Hence the lack of proper links on Instagram, and hence the "link in bio" workaround for those who still want to direct their audience offsite.) It is bad to have advertisements disrupt your reading of content; it is even worse if the content consists of advertisements. Seen from this perspective, there is a competition over

who gets to commodify Instagram: the corporation that owns the platform or the users who produce its content.

4. The digital humanities are another interdisciplinary field that has grown in response to digitization. Instead of merely looking for regularities, digital humanists have advanced forms of cultural inquiry that seek to contextualize their objects of study. Thus, the use of "distant reading" techniques to study digitized textual corpora or of "cultural analytics" for (often visual) cultural corpora are attuned to variation, and thus inherently require attention to context. Digital humanists, however, generally concern themselves with cultural objects (texts and images), and less with the people connected to them as authors or readers. As a result, they have relatively little to say about the social origins and effects of the cultural objects they study.
5. This story of this transformation is brilliantly told in Joanne McNeil's *Lurking* (2020).
6. This argument draws upon Jennifer Robinson's work on ordinary cities, which develops a postcolonial argument against the privileging of sites like Chicago, New York, or London for the development of theory and urges that any city can serve as a site for theorizing (Robinson 2013; see also Roy 2016).

Appendix

1. Chapter 4 is based on joint work with Laura Savolainen, which was published in *New Media & Society* (Savolainen, Uitermark, and Boy 2022). A previous version of Chapter 5 appeared in a special issue of *Social Media + Society* about Instagram (Boy and Uitermark 2020). Chapter 6 is adapted from joint work with Irene Bronsvoort published in *Urban Studies* (Bronsvoort and Uitermark 2022).
2. We used the Louvain method of modularity optimization (Blondel et al. 2008).

References

Chapter 1

Abidin, Crystal. 2018. *Internet Celebrity: Understanding Fame Online*. Bingley, UK: Emerald.

Abidin, Crystal. 2020. "Somewhere Between Here and There: Negotiating Researcher Visibility in a Digital Ethnography of the Influencer Industry." *Journal of Digital Social Research* 2, no. 1: 56–76. https://doi.org/10.33621/jdsr.v2i1.20.

Barabási, Albert L. 2002. *Linked: The New Science of Networks*. New York: Plume.

Barberá, Pablo, Ning Wang, Richard Bonneau, John T. Jost, Jonathan Nagler, Joshua Tucker, et al. 2015. "The Critical Periphery in the Growth of Social Protests." *PLOS ONE* 10, no. 11: 0143611. https://doi.org/10.1371/journal.pone.0143611.

Barinka, Alex. 2022. "Meta's Instagram Users Reach 2 Billion, Closing in on Facebook." *Bloomberg*, October. https://www.bloomberg.com/news/articles/2022-10-26/meta-s-instagram-users-reach-2-billion-closing-in-on-facebook.

Baym, Nancy K. 2015. *Personal Connections in the Digital Age*. New York: John Wiley & Sons.

Benkler, Yochai, Hal Roberts, Robert Faris, Alicia Solow-Niederman, and Bruce Etling. 2015. "Mobilization and the Networked Public Sphere: Mapping the SOPA–PIPA Debate." *Political Communication* 32, no. 4: 594–624. https://doi.org/10.1080/10584609.2014.986349.

Boterman, Willem, and Wouter van Gent. 2023. *Making the Middle-Class City: The Politics of Gentrifying Amsterdam*. New York: Palgrave Macmillan.

Boy, John D., and Justus Uitermark. 2016. "How to Study the City on Instagram." *PLOS ONE* 11, no. 6: 0158161. https://doi.org/10.1371/journal.pone.0158161.

Boy, John D., and Justus Uitermark. 2017. "Reassembling the City Through Instagram." *Transactions of the Institute of British Geographers* 42, no. 2: 612–624. https://doi.org/10.1111/tran.12185.

Brenner, Neil, and Christian Schmid. 2015. "Towards a New Epistemology of the Urban?" *City* 19, no. 2–3: 151–182. https://doi.org/10.1080/13604813.2015.1014712.

Burrell, Jenna. 2009. "The Field Site as a Network: A Strategy for Locating Ethnographic Research." *Field Methods* 21, no. 2: 181–199. https://doi.org/10.1177/1525822X08329699.

Castells, Manuel. 2012. *Networks of Outrage and Hope: Social Movements in the Internet Age*. Cambridge: Polity.

Couldry, Nick. 2012. *Media, Society, World: Social Theory and Digital Media Practice*. Cambridge: Polity.

Couldry, Nick. 2022. "The Social Construction of Reality—Really!" In *Social Media and Social Order*, edited by David Herbert and Stefan Fisher-Høyrem, 10–16. Berlin: De Gruyter.

Couldry, Nick, and Andreas Hepp. 2018. *The Mediated Construction of Reality*. Oxford: Wiley.

Currid-Halkett, Elizabeth. 2017. *The Sum of Small Things: A Theory of the Aspirational Class*. Princeton, NJ: Princeton University Press.

Dardot, Pierre, and Christian Laval. 2017. *The New Way of the World: On Neoliberal Society*. Translated by Gregory Elliott. London: Verso.

Duffy, Brooke Erin. 2017. *(Not) Getting Paid to Do What You Love: Gender, Social Media, and Aspirational Work*. New Haven, CT: Yale University Press.

Duneier, Mitch. 2011. "How Not to Lie with Ethnography." *Sociological Methodology* 41, no. 1: 1–11. https://doi.org/10.1111/j.1467-9531.2011.01249.x.

Flyvbjerg, Bent. 2006. "Five Misunderstandings about Case-Study Research." *Qualitative Inquiry* 12, no. 2: 219–245. https://doi.org/10.1177/1077800405284363.

González-Bailón, Sandra, and Ning Wang. 2016. "Networked Discontent: The Anatomy of Protest Campaigns in Social Media." *Social Networks* 44: 95–104. https://doi.org/10.1016/j.socnet.2015.07.003.

Halegoua, Germaine R. 2020. *The Digital City: Media and the Social Production of Place*. New York: NYU Press.

Herbert, David, and Stefan Fisher-Høyrem, eds. 2022. *Social Media and Social Order*. Berlin: De Gruyter.

Hoekstra, Hans, Tim Jonker, and Neil van der Veer. 2023. "Nationale Social Media Onderzoek." Amsterdam: Newcom Research & Consultancy.

Lane, Jeffrey. 2018. *The Digital Street*. New York: Oxford University Press.

Lane, Jeffrey, and Will Marler. 2020. "Networked Street Life." In *The Oxford Handbook of Sociology and Digital Media*, edited by Deana A. Rohlinger and Sarah Sobieraj, 443–466. New York: Oxford University Press. https://doi.org/10.1093/oxfordhb/9780197510636.013.41.

Leaver, Tama, Tim Highfield, and Crystal Abidin. 2020. *Instagram: Visual Social Media Cultures*. New York: Wiley.

Manovich, Lev. 2017. "Instagram and Contemporary Image." http://manovich.net/index.php/projects/instagram-and-contemporary-image.

Marwick, Alice E. 2013. *Status Update: Celebrity, Publicity, and Branding in the Social Media Age*. New Haven, CT: Yale University Press.
Postman, Neil. 2010. "Five Things We Need to Know about Technological Change." In *Computers in Society*, 15th ed., edited by Paul De Palma, 3–6. New York: McGraw Hill.
Rohlinger, Deana A. 2019. *New Media and Society*. New York: NYU Press.
Schradie, Jen. 2011. "The Digital Production Gap: The Digital Divide and Web 2.0 Collide." *Poetics* 39, no. 2: 145–168. https://doi.org/10.1016/j.poetic.2011.02.003.
Simmel, Georg. 2021. "The Metropolis and the Life of Spirit: A New Translation." Translated by John D. Boy. *Journal of Classical Sociology* 21, no. 2: 188–202. https://doi.org/10.1177/1468795X20980638.
Stevenson, Seth. 2018. "Instagram's Kevin Systrom on the Platform He Built for One Billion Users." *WSJ Magazine*, September.
van Deursen, Alexander J. A. M., and Jan A. G. M. van Dijk. 2014. "The Digital Divide Shifts to Differences in Usage." *New Media & Society* 16, no. 3: 507–526. https://doi.org/10.1177/1461444813487959.
Wachsmuth, David. 2014. "City as Ideology: Reconciling the Explosion of the City Form with the Tenacity of the City Concept." *Environment and Planning D* 31: 75–90. https://doi.org/10.1068/d21911.

Chapter 2

Abidin, Crystal. 2016a. "'Aren't These Just Young, Rich Women Doing Vain Things Online?': Influencer Selfies as Subversive Frivolity." *Social Media + Society* 2, no. 2: 1–17. https://doi.org/10.1177/2056305116641342.
Abidin, Crystal. 2016b. "Visibility Labour: Engaging with Influencers' Fashion Brands and #OOTD Advertorial Campaigns on Instagram." *Media International Australia* 161, no. 1: 86–100. https://doi.org/10.1177/1329878X16665177.
Adamic, Lada A., and Natalie Glance. 2005. "The Political Blogosphere and the 2004 U.S. Election: Divided They Blog." In LinkKDD '05: *Proceedings of the 3rd International Workshop on Link Discovery, August 2005*, edited by Jafar Adibi, 36–43. New York: Association for Computing Machinery. https://doi.org/10.1145/1134271.1134277.
Aral, Sinan. 2020. *The Hype Machine: How Social Media Disrupts Our Elections, Our Economy, and Our Health—and How We Must Adapt*. New York: Currency.
Archer, Margaret S. 2007. *Making Our Way Through the World: Human Reflexivity and Social Mobility*. Cambridge: Cambridge University Press.
Arendt, Hannah. 1958. *The Human Condition*. Chicago: University of Chicago Press.

Bail, Chris. 2021. *Breaking the Social Media Prism: How to Make Our Platforms Less Polarizing*. Princeton, NJ: Princeton University Press.

Barns, Sarah. 2019. *Platform Urbanism: Negotiating Platform Ecosystems in Connected Cities*. Berlin: Springer.

Beck, Ulrich, Anthony Giddens, and Scott Lash. 1994. *Reflexive Modernization: Politics, Tradition and Aesthetics in the Modern Social Order*. Stanford: Stanford University Press.

Benkler, Yochai. 2007. *The Wealth of Networks: How Social Production Transforms Markets and Freedom*. New Haven, CT: Yale University Press.

Berger, John. 1972. *Ways of Seeing*. London: Penguin.

Beveridge, Ross, and Philippe Koch. 2023. *How Cities Can Transform Democracy*. Cambridge: Polity.

Bishop, Sophie. 2022. "Influencer Creep: Self-Documenting and Self-Branding Are Becoming Basic to All Forms of Work." *Real Life*, June. https://reallifemag.com/influencer-creep/.

Bourdieu, Pierre. 1984. *Distinction: A Social Critique of the Judgement of Taste*. Translated by Richard Nice. Cambridge, MA: Harvard University Press.

Bourdieu, Pierre. 2000. *Pascalian Meditations*. Translated by Richard Nice. Stanford, CA: Stanford University Press.

Bourdieu, Pierre, Luc Boltanski, Robert Castel, Jean-Claude Chamboredon, and Dominique Schnapper. 1990. *Photography: A Middle-Brow Art*. Translated by Shaun Whiteside. Stanford, CA: Stanford University Press.

Caliandro, Alessandro, and James Graham. 2020. "Studying Instagram Beyond Selfies." *Social Media + Society* 6, no. 2. https://doi.org/10.1177/2056305120924779.

Castells, Manuel. 2009. *Communication Power*. New York: Oxford University Press.

Collins, Randall. 2004. *Interaction Ritual Chains*. Princeton, NJ: Princeton University Press.

Cooley, Charles Horton. 1956. *The Two Major Works of Charles H. Cooley: Social Organization and Human Nature and the Social Order*. Glencoe, IL: The Free Press.

Couldry, Nick. 2012. *Media, Society, World: Social Theory and Digital Media Practice*. Cambridge: Polity.

Dean, Jodi. 2002. *Publicity's Secret: How Technoculture Capitalizes on Democracy*. Ithaca, NY: Cornell University Press.

Dean, Jodi. 2003. "Why the Net Is Not a Public Sphere." *Constellations* 10, no. 1: 95–112. https://doi.org/10.1111/1467-8675.00315.

Degen, Mónica Montserrat, and Gillian Rose. 2022. *The New Urban Aesthetic: Digital Experiences of Urban Change*. London: Bloomsbury.

de Swaan, Abram. 2001. *Human Societies: An Introduction*. Translated by Beverley Jackson. Cambridge: Polity.

Diehl, Kristin, Gal Zauberman, and Alixandra Barasch. 2016. "How Taking Photos Increases Enjoyment of Experiences." *Journal of Personality and Social Psychology* 111, no. 2: 119–140. https://doi.org/10.1037/pspa0000055.

Duffy, Brooke Erin. 2017. *(Not) Getting Paid to Do What You Love: Gender, Social Media, and Aspirational Work*. New Haven, CT: Yale University Press.

Duffy, Brooke Erin, and Emily Hund. 2015. "'Having It All' on Social Media: Entrepreneurial Femininity and Self-Branding Among Fashion Bloggers." *Social Media + Society* 1, no. 2. https://doi.org/10.1177/20563 05115604337.

Elias, Norbert. 1983. *The Court Society*. Translated by Edmund Jephcott. Oxford: Blackwell.

Elias, Norbert. 1991a. *The Society of Individuals*. Translated by Edmund Jephcott. Oxford: Blackwell.

Elias, Norbert. 1991b. *The Symbol Theory*. Edited by Richard Kilminster. London: Sage.

Elias, Norbert. 1994. *The Civilizing Process: Sociogenetic and Psychogenetic Investigations*. Vol. 2. Translated by Edwin Jephcott. Oxford: Blackwell.

Foucault, Michel. 1979. *The History of Sexuality*. Vol. 1. London: Allen Lane.

Gandini, Alessandro. 2016. *The Reputation Economy: Understanding Knowledge Work in Digital Society*. Basingstoke: Palgrave Macmillan.

Giddens, Anthony. 1991. *Modernity and Self-Identity: Self and Society in the Late Modern Age*. Palo Alto, CA: Stanford University Press.

Goffman, Erving. 1959. *The Presentation of Self in Everyday Life*. London: Penguin.

Goffman, Erving. 1979. *Gender Advertisements*. London: Macmillan.

Goffman, Erving. 1986. *Stigma: Notes on the Management of Spoiled Identity*. New York: Simon & Schuster.

Graham, Mark, Matthew Zook, and Andrew Boulton. 2013. "Augmented Reality in Urban Places: Contested Content and the Duplicity of Code." *Transactions of the Institute of British Geographers* 38, no. 3: 464–479. https://doi.org/10.1111/j.1475-5661.2012.00539.x.

Granovetter, Mark. 1973. "The Strength of Weak Ties." *American Journal of Sociology* 78, no. 6: 1360–1380. https://doi.org/10.1086/225469.

Habermas, Jürgen. 1991. *The Structural Transformation of the Public Sphere: An Inquiry into a Category of Bourgeois Society*. Translated by Thomas Burger. Cambridge, MA: MIT Press.

Habermas, Jürgen. 2006. "Ein avantgardistischer Spürsinn für Relevanzen: Was den Intellektuellen auszeichnet." *Blätter für deutsche und internationale Politik* 51, no. 5: 551–557.

Halegoua, Germaine R. 2020. *The Digital City: Media and the Social Production of Place*. New York: NYU Press.

Harari, Yuval Noah. 2015. *Sapiens: A Brief History of Humankind*. New York: HarperCollins.

Harris, Malcolm. 2017. *Kids These Days: Human Capital and the Making of Millennials*. Boston: Little, Brown.

Hepp, Andreas. 2010. "Researching 'Mediatised Worlds': Non-Media-Centric Media and Communication Research as a Challenge." In *Media and Communication Studies: Intersections and Interventions*, edited by Nico Carpentier, Ilija Tomanić Trivundža, Pille Pruulmann-Vengerfeldt, Ebba Sundin, Tobias Olsson, and Richard Kilborn, 37–48. Tartu: Tartu University Press.

Kolbert, Elizabeth. 2017. "Why Facts Don't Change Our Minds." *The New Yorker*, February 27. https://www.newyorker.com/magazine/2017/02/27/why-facts-dont-change-our-minds.

Kotsko, Adam. 2017. "Jury Duty: How the Internet Became a Tool for Judgment Rather Than Dialogue." *Real Life*, January. http://reallifemag.com/jury-duty/.

Krajina, Zlatan, and Deborah Stevenson, eds. 2020. *The Routledge Companion to Urban Media and Communication*. London: Routledge.

Lasch, Christopher. 1979. *The Culture of Narcissism: American Life in an Age of Diminishing Expectations*. New York: Norton.

Leszczynski, Agnieska. 2020. "Glitchy Vignettes of Platform Urbanism." *Environment and Planning D* 38, no. 2: 189–208. https://doi.org/10.1177/0263775819878721.

Livingstone, Sonia. 2009. *Children and the Internet*. Cambridge: Polity.

Losse, Katherine. 2012. *The Boy Kings: A Journey into the Heart of the Social Network*. New York: Free Press.

Low, Setha. 2016. *Spatializing Culture: The Ethnography of Space and Place*. London: Routledge.

MacIsaac, Sarah, J. Kelly, and S. Gray. 2018. "'She Has Like 4,000 Followers!': The Celebrification of Self Within School Social Networks." *Journal of Youth Studies* 21, no. 6: 816–835. https://doi.org/10.1080/13676261.2017.1420764.

Mackson, Samantha B., Paula M. Brochu, and Barry A. Schneider. 2019. "Instagram: Friend or Foe? The Application's Association with Psychological Well-Being." *New Media & Society* 21, no. 10: 2160–2182. https://doi.org/10.1177/1461444819840021.

Manovich, Lev. 2020. *Cultural Analytics*. Cambridge, MA: MIT Press.

Marwick, Alice E. 2013. *Status Update: Celebrity, Publicity, and Branding in the Social Media Age*. New Haven, CT: Yale University Press.

Marwick, Alice E. 2015. "Instafame: Luxury Selfies in the Attention Economy." *Public Culture* 27, no. 1: 137–160. https://doi.org/10.1215/08992363-2798379.

Marwick, Alice E. 2018. "Why Do People Share Fake News? A Sociotechnical Model of Media Effects." *Georgetown Law Technology Review* 2, no. 2: 474–512.

Mau, Steffen. 2019. *The Metric Society: On the Quantification of the Social*. Translated by Sharon Howe. Cambridge: Polity.

Milner, Murray, Jr. 2016. *Freaks, Geeks, and Cool Kids: Teenagers in an Era of Consumerism, Standardized Tests and Social Media*. 2nd ed. New York: Routledge.

Mirzoeff, Nicholas. 2015. *How to See the World*. London: Pelican.

Morley, David. 2009. "For a Materialist, Non-Media-Centric Media Studies." *Television & New Media* 10, no. 1: 114–116. https://doi.org/10.1177/1527476408327173.

O'Neil, Kathy. 2022. *The Shame Machine: Who Profits in the New Age of Humiliation*. New York: Crown.

Papacharissi, Zizi. 2002. "The Virtual Sphere: The Internet as a Public Sphere." *New Media & Society* 4, no. 1: 9–27. https://doi.org/10.1177/14614440222226244.

Piketty, Thomas. 2014. *Capital in the Twenty-First Century*. Cambridge, MA: Harvard University Press.

Postman, Neil. 2010. "Five Things We Need to Know about Technological Change." In *Computers in Society*, 15th ed., edited by Paul De Palma, 3–6. New York: McGraw Hill.

Reagle, Joseph. 2015. *Reading the Comments: Likers, Haters, and the Manipulators at the Bottom of the Web*. Cambridge, MA: MIT Press.

Ridgeway, Cecilia L. 2019. *Status: Why Is It Everywhere? Why Does It Matter?* New York: Russell Sage Foundation.

Rodgers, Scott, and Susan Moore, eds. 2018. "Platform Urbanism." *Mediapolis*. https://www.mediapolisjournal.com/roundtables/platform-urbanism/.

Rogers, Richard. 2016. "Otherwise Engaged: Social Media from Vanity Metrics to Critical Analytics." *International Journal of Communication* 12: 450–472.

Rose, Gillian. 2022. "Introduction: Seeing the City Digitally." In *Seeing the City Digitally: Processing Urban Space and Time*, edited by Gillian Rose, 9–33. Amsterdam: Amsterdam University Press.

Rose, Gillian, Parvati Raghuram, Sophie Watson, and Edward Wigley. 2021. "Platform Urbanism, Smartphone Applications and Valuing Data in a Smart City." *Transactions of the Institute of British Geographers* 46, no. 1: 59–72. https://doi.org/10.1111/tran.12400.

Sadowski, Jathan. 2020. *Too Smart: How Digital Capitalism Is Extracting Data, Controlling Our Lives, and Taking over the World*. Cambridge, MA: MIT Press.

Scolere, Leah, Urszula Pruchniewska, and Brooke Erin Duffy. 2018. "Constructing the Platform-Specific Self-Brand: The Labor of Social Media Promotion." *Social Media + Society* 4, no. 3. https://doi.org/10.1177/2056305118784768.

Senft, Theresa M. 2020. "Hating Habermas: On Exhibitionism, Shame, and Life on the Actually Existing Internet." In *Photography Reframed: New*

Visions in Contemporary Photographic Culture, edited by Ben Burbridge and Annebella Pollen, 108–115. Abingdon: Routledge.
Senft, Theresa M., and Nancy K. Baym. 2015. "What Does the Selfie Say? Investigating a Global Phenomenon." *International Journal of Communication* 9: 1588–1606. https://ijoc.org/index.php/ijoc/article/view/4067/1387.
Shelton, Taylor, Ate Poorthuis, and Matthew Zook. 2015. "Social Media and the City: Rethinking Urban Socio-Spatial Inequality Using User-Generated Geographic Information." *Landscape and Urban Planning* 142: 198–211. https://doi.org/10.1016/j.landurbplan.2015.02.020.
Srnicek, Nick. 2017. *Platform Capitalism*. Cambridge: Polity.
Vaidhyanathan, Siva. 2018. *Antisocial Media: How Facebook Disconnects Us and Undermines Democracy*. New York: Oxford University Press.
Valkenburg, Patti M., and Jessica Taylor Piotrowski. 2017. *Plugged In: How Media Attract and Affect Youth*. New Haven, CT: Yale University Press.
van Doorn, Niels. 2017. "Platform Labor: On the Gendered and Racialized Exploitation of Low-Income Service Work in the 'on-Demand' Economy." *Information, Communication & Society* 20, no. 6: 898–914. https://doi.org/10.1080/1369118X.2017.1294194.
van Doorn, Niels. 2020. "A New Institution on the Block: On Platform Urbanism and Airbnb Citizenship." *New Media & Society* 22, no. 10: 1808–1826. https://doi.org/10.1177/1461444819884377.
Veblen, Thorstein. 1934. *The Theory of the Leisure Class: An Economic Study of Institutions*. New York: The Modern Library.
Wachsmuth, David, and Alexander Weisler. 2018. "Airbnb and the Rent Gap: Gentrification Through the Sharing Economy." *Environment and Planning A* 50, no. 6: 1147–1170. https://doi.org/10.1177/0308518X18778038.
Williams, Raymond. 1975. *Television: Technology and Cultural Form*. New York: Schocken.
Wouters, Cas. 2007. *Informalization: Manners and Emotions Since 1890*. London: Sage.
Zhang, Renwen. 2017. "The Stress-Buffering Effect of Self-Disclosure on Facebook: An Examination of Stressful Life Events, Social Support, and Mental Health Among College Students." *Computers in Human Behavior* 75: 527–537. https://doi.org/10.1016/j.chb.2017.05.043.

Chapter 3

Ahmed, Sara. 2010. *The Promise of Happiness*. Durham, NC: Duke University Press.

Andalibi, Nazanin, Pinar Ozturk, and Andrea Forte. 2015. "Depression-Related Imagery on Instagram." In *CSCW'15 Companion: Proceedings of the 18th ACM Conference Companion on Computer Supported Cooperative Work & Social Computing*, edited by Luigina Ciolfi and David McDonal, 231–234. New York: Association for Computing Machinery. https://doi.org/10.1145/2685553.2699014.

Andalibi, Nazanin, Pinar Ozturk, and Andrea Forte. 2017. "Sensitive Self-Disclosures, Responses, and Social Support on Instagram: The Case of #Depression." In *CSCW'17: Proceedings of the 2017 ACM Conference Companion on Computer Supported Cooperative Work & Social Computing*, edited by Louise Barkhuus, Marcos Borges, and Wendy Kellogg, 1485–1500. New York: Association for Computing Machinery. https://doi.org/10.1145/2998181.2998243.

Berryman, Rachel, and Misha Kavka. 2018. "Crying on YouTube: Vlogs, Self-Exposure and the Productivity of Negative Affect." *Convergence* 24, no. 1: 85–98. https://doi.org/10.1177/1354856517736981.

Beyens, Ine, J. Loes Pouwels, Irene I. van Driel, Loes Keijsers, and Patti M. Valkenburg. 2020. "The Effect of Social Media on Well-Being Differs from Adolescent to Adolescent." *Scientific Reports* 10, no. 1: 10763. https://doi.org/10.1038/s41598-020-67727-7.

Bollen, John, Bruno Gonçalves, Ingrid Leemput, and Guangchen Ruan. 2017. "The Happiness Paradox: Your Friends Are Happier Than You." *EPJ Data Science* 6, no. 4: 1–10. https://doi.org/10.1140/epjds/s13688-017-0100-1.

Bucher, Taina. 2018. *If . . . Then: Algorithmic Power and Politics*. New York: Oxford University Press.

Bucher, Taina. 2021. *Facebook*. Cambridge: Polity.

Chatzopoulou, Elena, Raffaele Filieri, and Shannon Arzu Dogruyol. 2020. "Instagram and Body Image: Motivation to Conform to the 'Instabod' and Consequences on Young Male Wellbeing." *The Journal of Consumer Affairs* 54, no. 4: 1270–1297. https://doi.org/10.1111/joca.12329.

Cottingham, Marci D. 2022. *Practical Feelings: Emotions as Resources in a Dynamic Social World*. New York: Oxford University Press.

de Vries, Dian A., A. Marthe Möller, Marieke S. Wieringa, Anniek W. Eigenraam, and Kirsten Hamelink. 2018. "Social Comparison as the Thief of Joy: Emotional Consequences of Viewing Strangers' Instagram Posts." *Media Psychology* 21, no. 2: 222–245. https://doi.org/10.1080/15213269.2016.1267647.

Dredge, Rebecca, and Lara Schreurs. 2020. "Social Media Use and Offline Interpersonal Outcomes During Youth: A Systematic Literature Review." *Mass Communication and Society* 23, no. 6: 885–911. https://doi.org/10.1080/15205436.2020.1810277.

Feld, Scott L. 1991. "Why Your Friends Have More Friends Than You Do." *American Journal of Sociology* 96, no. 6: 1464–1477. https://doi.org/10.1086/229693.

Fiers, Floor. 2020. "Hiding Traces of Status Seeking: Contradictory Tagging Strategies on Instagram." *Social Media + Society* 6, no. 2. https://doi.org/10.1177/2056305120937318.

Giddens, Anthony. 1991. *Modernity and Self-Identity: Self and Society in the Late Modern Age*. Palo Alto, CA: Stanford University Press.

Grund, Thomas U. 2014. "Why Your Friends Are More Important and Special Than You Think." *Sociological Science* 1: 128–140. https://doi.org/10.15195/v1.a10.

Kay, Jonah. 2020. "The Evolution of Instagram Activism." *Hyperallergic*, October. https://hyperallergic.com/597846/the-evolution-of-instagram-activism/.

King, Vera. 2020. "'Lots of People Pretend . . .': Shame Conflicts in an Age of Digital Self-Presentation and Point-Scoring." *Beijing International Review of Education* 2, no. 3: 388–402. https://doi.org/10.1163/25902539-00203006.

Krogh, Søren Christian. 2023. "'You Can't Do Anything Right': How Adolescents Experience and Navigate the Achievement Imperative on Social Media." *Young* 31, no. 1: 5–21. https://doi.org/10.1177/11033088221111224.

MacIsaac, Sarah, J. Kelly, and S. Gray. 2018. "'She Has Like 4,000 Followers!': The Celebrification of Self Within School Social Networks." *Journal of Youth Studies* 21, no. 6: 816–835. https://doi.org/10.1080/13676261.2017.1420764.

Marwick, Alice E. 2013. *Status Update: Celebrity, Publicity, and Branding in the Social Media Age*. New Haven, CT: Yale University Press.

Marwick, Alice E., and Nicole B. Ellison. 2012. "'There Isn't Wifi in Heaven!': Negotiating Visibility on Facebook Memorial Pages." *Journal of Broadcasting & Electronic Media* 56, no. 3: 378–400. https://doi.org/10.1080/08838151.2012.705197.

Orben, Amy, Tobias Dienlin, and Andrew K. Przybylski. 2019. "Social Media's Enduring Effect on Adolescent Life Satisfaction." *PNAS* 116, no. 21: 10226–10228. https://doi.org/10.1073/pnas.1902058116.

Peute, Marije, and Annemarije Rus. 2021. "Displays of Vanity on Instagram: Reflection on the Making of *Instaworthy*." *Etnofoor* 33, no. 1: 11–20.

Twenge, Jean M. 2017. *iGen: Why Today's Super-Connected Kids Are Growing up Less Rebellious, More Tolerant, Less Happy—and Completely Unprepared for Adulthood*. New York: Simon & Schuster.

Valkenburg, Patti M., and Jessica Taylor Piotrowski. 2017. *Plugged In: How Media Attract and Affect Youth*. New Haven, CT: Yale University Press.

Zhou, Xinyi, Shengmin Jin, and Reza Zafarani. 2020. "Sentiment Paradoxes in Social Networks: Why Your Friends Are More Positive Than You?" Proceedings of the International AAAI Conference on Web and Social Media 14, no. 1: 798–807. https://doi.org/10.1609/icwsm.v14i1.7344.

Chapter 4

Ahmed, Sara. 2017. *Living a Feminist Life*. Durham, NC: Duke University Press.

Banet-Weiser, Sarah. 2018. *Empowered: Popular Feminism and Popular Misogyny*. Durham, NC: Duke University Press.

Baym, Nancy K. 2015. "Connect with Your Audience! The Relational Labor of Connection." *The Communication Review* 18, no. 1: 14–22. https://doi.org/10.1080/10714421.2015.996401.

Caldeira, Sofia P., Sander De Ridder, and Sofie Van Bauwel. 2020. "Between the Mundane and the Political: Women's Self-Representations on Instagram." *Social Media + Society* 6, no. 3. https://doi.org/10.1177/2056305120940802.

Davis, Jenny L. 2014. "Triangulating the Self: Identity Processes in a Connected Era." *Symbolic Interaction* 37, no. 4: 500–523. https://doi.org/10.1002/symb.123.

Duffy, Brooke Erin, and Elizabeth Wissinger. 2017. "Mythologies of Creative Work in the Social Media Age: Fun, Free, and 'Just Being Me.'" *International Journal of Communication* 11: 20. https://ijoc.org/index.php/ijoc/article/view/7322.

Leaver, Tama, Tim Highfield, and Crystal Abidin. 2020. *Instagram: Visual Social Media Cultures*. New York: Wiley.

Manovich, Lev. 2013. *Software Takes Command*. London: Bloomsbury.

Mohanty, Chandra Talpade. 1984. "Under Western Eyes: Feminist Scholarship and Colonial Discourses." *Boundary 2* 12/13: 333–358. https://doi.org/10.2307/302821.

Norman, Donald A. 1988. *The Psychology of Everyday Things*. New York: Basic.

Poell, Thomas, David Nieborg, and Brooke Erin Duffy. 2021. *Platforms and Cultural Production*. Cambridge: Polity.

Prügl, Elisabeth. 2015. "Neoliberalising Feminism." *New Political Economy* 20, no. 4: 614–631. https://doi.org/10.1080/13563467.2014.951614.

Savolainen, Laura, Justus Uitermark, and John D. Boy. 2022. "Filtering Feminisms: Emergent Feminist Visibilities on Instagram." *New Media & Society* 24, no. 3: 557–579. https://doi.org/10.1177/1461444820960074.

Tolentino, Jia. 2019. *Trick Mirror: Reflections on Self-Delusion*. London: 4th Estate.

Chapter 5

Boy, John D., and Justus Uitermark. 2016. "How to Study the City on Instagram." *PLOS ONE* 11, no. 6: 0158161. https://doi.org/10.1371/journal.pone.0158161.

Boy, John D., and Justus Uitermark. 2017. "Reassembling the City Through Instagram." *Transactions of the Institute of British Geographers* 42, no. 2: 612–624. https://doi.org/10.1111/tran.12185.

Butler, Tim, and Garry Robson. 2001. "Coming to Terms with London: Middle Class Communities in a Global City." *International Journal of Urban and Regional Research* 25, no. 1: 70–86. https://doi.org/10.1111/1468-2427.00298.

Caliandro, Alessandro, and James Graham. 2020. "Studying Instagram Beyond Selfies." *Social Media + Society* 6, no. 2. https://doi.org/10.1177/2056305120924779.

Chayka, Kyle. 2016. "Welcome to Airspace: How Silicon Valley Helps Spread the Same Sterile Aesthetic Across the World." *The Verge*, August. https://www.theverge.com/2016/8/3/12325104/airbnb-aesthetic-global-minimalism-startup-gentrification.

CityLab Staff. 2017. "Your Entire City Is an Instagram Playground Now." *CityLab*, December. https://www.citylab.com/design/2017/12/congrats-your-city-is-an-instagram-playground-now/549152/.

Costa, Elisabetta. 2018. "Affordances-in-Practice: An Ethnographic Critique of Social Media Logic and Context Collapse." *New Media & Society* 20, no. 10: 3641–3656. https://doi.org/10.1177/1461444818756290.

Currid-Halkett, Elizabeth. 2017. *The Sum of Small Things: A Theory of the Aspirational Class*. Princeton, NJ: Princeton University Press.

de Waal, Martijn. 2014. *The City as Interface: How Digital Media Are Changing the City*. Rotterdam: Nai010.

Elias, Norbert. 1983. *The Court Society*. Translated by Edmund Jephcott. Oxford: Blackwell.

Elias, Norbert. 1994. *The Civilizing Process: Sociogenetic and Psychogenetic Investigations, vol. 2*. Translated by Edwin Jephcott. Oxford: Blackwell.

Graham, Stephen. 2005. "Software-Sorted Geographies." *Progress in Human Geography* 29, no. 5: 562–580. https://doi.org/10.1191/0309132505ph568oa.

Hochman, Nadav, and Lev Manovich. 2013. "Zooming into an Instagram City: Reading the Local Through Social Media." *First Monday* 18, no. 7. https://doi.org/10.5210/fm.v18i7.4711.

Jackson, Emma, and Tim Butler. 2015. "Revisiting 'Social Tectonics': The Middle Classes and Social Mix in Gentrifying Neighbourhoods." *Urban Studies* 52, no. 13: 2349–2365. https://doi.org/10.1177/0042098014547370.

Leszczynski, Agnieszka, and Vivian Kong. 2022. "Gentrification and the An/Aesthetics of Digital Spatial Capital in Canadian 'Platform Cities.'" *The Canadian Geographer/Le Géographe canadien* 66, no. 1: 8–22. https://doi.org/10.1111/cag.12726.

Lindell, Johan, André Jansson, and Karin Fast. 2021. "I'm Here! Conspicuous Geomedia Practices and the Reproduction of Social Positions on Social Media." *Information, Communication & Society* 25, no. 14: 2063–2082. https://doi.org/10.1080/1369118x.2021.1925322.

Lingel, Jessa. 2017. *Digital Countercultures and the Struggle for Community*. Cambridge, MA: MIT Press.

Lofland, Lyn H. 1998. *The Public Realm: Exploring the City's Quintessential Social Territory*. New York: Aldine De Gruyter.

Marwick, Alice E. 2013. *Status Update: Celebrity, Publicity, and Branding in the Social Media Age*. New Haven, CT: Yale University Press.

Marwick, Alice E., and Danah Boyd. 2010. "I Tweet Honestly, I Tweet Passionately: Twitter Users, Context Collapse, and the Imagined Audience." *New Media & Society* 13, no. 1: 114–133. https://doi.org/10.1177/1461444810365313.

Matchar, Emily. 2017. "How Instagram Is Changing the Way We Design Cultural Spaces." *Smithsonian Magazine*, November. https://www.smithsonianmag.com/innovation/how-instagram-changing-way-we-design-cultural-spaces-180967071/.

Pariser, Eli. 2011. *The Filter Bubble: What the Internet Is Hiding from You*. New York: Penguin.

Pelly, Liz. 2019. "The Antisocial Network." *Logic Magazine*, no. 6, January. https://logicmag.io/play/the-antisocial-network/.

Rogers, Richard. 2020. "Deplatforming: Following Extreme Internet Celebrities to Telegram and Alternative Social Media." *European Journal of Communication* 35, no. 3: 213–229. https://doi.org/10.1177/0267323120922066.

Schep, Tijmen. 2017. "Social Cooling." http://www.socialcooling.com/.

Silver, Daniel, and Terry Nichols Clark. 2016. *Scenescapes: How Qualities of Place Shape Social Life*. Chicago: University of Chicago Press.

Sunstein, Cass R. 2001. *Republic.com*. Princeton, NJ: Princeton University Press.

Thornton, Sarah. 1996. *Club Cultures: Music, Media, and Subcultural Capital*. Middletown, CT: Wesleyan University Press.

Turner, Bryan S. 2011. *Religion and Modern Society: Citizenship, Secularisation and the State*. Cambridge: Cambridge University Press.

Veblen, Thorstein. 1934. *The Theory of the Leisure Class: An Economic Study of Institutions*. New York: The Modern Library.

Wang, Qi, Nolan E. Phillips, Mario Small, and Robert J. Sampson. 2018. "Urban Mobility and Neighborhood Isolation in America's 50 Largest Cities." *PNAS* 115, no. 30: 7735–7740. https://doi.org/10.1073/pnas.1802537115.

Zasina, Jakub. 2018. "The Instagram Image of the City: Insights from Łódź, Poland." *Bulletin of Geography: Socio-Economic Series* 42, no. 42: 213–225. https://doi.org/10.2478/bog-2018-0040.

Chapter 6

Bronsvoort, Irene, and Justus L. Uitermark. 2022. "Seeing the Street Through Instagram: Digital Platforms and the Amplification of Gentrification." *Urban Studies* 59, no. 14: 2857–2874. https://doi.org/10.1177/0042098021 1046539.

Degen, Mónica Montserrat, and Gillian Rose. 2022. *The New Urban Aesthetic: Digital Experiences of Urban Change*. London: Bloomsbury.

Halegoua, Germaine R. 2020. *The Digital City: Media and the Social Production of Place*. New York: NYU Press.

Hampton, Keith N. 2016. "Persistent and Pervasive Community: New Communication Technologies and the Future of Community." *American Behavioral Scientist* 60, no. 1: 101–124. https://doi.org/10.1177/000276421 5601714.

Leaver, Tama, Tim Highfield, and Crystal Abidin. 2020. *Instagram: Visual Social Media Cultures*. Oxford: Wiley.

Manovich, Lev. 2017. "Instagram and Contemporary Image." http://manovich.net/index.php/projects/instagram-and-contemporary-image.

Pinkster, Fenne M., and Willem R. Boterman. 2017. "When the Spell Is Broken: Gentrification, Urban Tourism and Privileged Discontent in the Amsterdam Canal District." *Cultural Geographies* 24, no. 3: 457–472. https://doi.org/10.1177/1474474017706176.

Sakızlıoğlu, Bahar, and Loretta Lees. 2020. "Commercial Gentrification, Ethnicity, and Social Mixedness: The Case of Javastraat, Indische Buurt, Amsterdam." *City & Community* 19, 4: 870–889. https://doi.org/10.1111/cico.12451.

Savage, Mike, Gaynor Bagnall, and Brian Longhurst. 2005. *Globalization and Belonging*. London: SAGE.

Schoemaker, Jacqueline. 2017. *Het failliet van de Javastraat*. Amsterdam: Editie Leesmagazijn.

Smidt, Having Sjoerd. 2015. "Gentrificatie in Amsterdam Oost: Kwalitatief onderzoek naar de invloed van de gemeente op de rol van horeca in stadsdeel Amsterdam Oost." BA thesis, University of Amsterdam.

Smit, Maxime. 2016. "Oost vs. West: waar gebeurt hét?" *Het Parool*, January.

Smit, Maxime. 2017. *De Javastraat: Biografie van een volksstraat*. Amsterdam: Atlas Contact.
van Eck, Emil, Iris Hagemans, and Jan Rath. 2020. "The Ambiguity of Diversity: Management of Ethnic and Class Transitions in a Gentrifying Local Shopping Street." *Urban Studies* 57, no. 16: 3299–3314. https://doi.org/10.1177/0042098019897008.
Zukin, Sharon. 1995. *The Cultures of Cities*. Oxford: Wiley.
Zukin, Sharon, Philip Kasinitz, and Xiangming Chen, eds. 2015. *Global Cities, Local Streets: Everyday Diversity from New York to Shanghai*. London: Routledge.
Zukin, Sharon, Scarlett Lindeman, and Laurie Hurson. 2017. "The Omnivore's Neighborhood? Online Restaurant Reviews, Race, and Gentrification." *Journal of Consumer Culture* 17, 3: 459–479. https://doi.org/10.1177/1469540515611203.

Chapter 7

Abidin, Crystal. 2017. "#Familygoals: Family Influencers, Calibrated Amateurism, and Justifying Young Digital Labor." *Social Media + Society* 3, no. 2. https://doi.org/10.1177/2056305117707191.
Berry, Jeffrey M., and Sarah Sobieraj. 2016. *The Outrage Industry: Political Opinion Media and the New Incivility*. Oxford: Oxford University Press.
Bourdieu, Pierre. 1990. *The Logic of Practice*. Stanford, CA: Stanford University Press.
Boy, John D., and Justus Uitermark. 2017. "Reassembling the City Through Instagram." *Transactions of the Institute of British Geographers* 42, no. 2: 612–624. https://doi.org/10.1111/tran.12185.
Boy, John D., and Justus Uitermark. 2022. "The Dramaturgy of Social Media: Platform Ecology, Uneven Networks, and the Myth of the Self." In *Social Media and Social Order*, edited by David Herbert and Stefan Fisher-Høyrem, 17–32. Berlin: De Gruyter.
Bucher, Taina, and Anne Helmond. 2017. "The Affordances of Social Media Platforms." In *The SAGE Handbook of Social Media*, edited by Jean Burgess, Thomas Poell, and Alice E. Marwick, 233–253. London: SAGE.
Cohen, Peter D. A. 2000. "Is the Addiction Doctor the Voodoo Priest of Western Man?" *Addiction Research* 8, no. 6: 589–598. https://doi.org/10.3109/16066350008998990.
Couldry, Nick. 2012. *Media, Society, World: Social Theory and Digital Media Practice*. Cambridge: Polity.
Davis, Jenny L. 2020. *How Artifacts Afford: The Power and Politics of Everyday Things*. Cambridge, MA: MIT Press.

de Swaan, Abram. 2001. *Human Societies: An Introduction*. Translated by Beverley Jackson. Cambridge: Polity.

Duffy, Brooke Erin. 2017. *(Not) Getting Paid to Do What You Love: Gender, Social Media, and Aspirational Work*. New Haven, CT: Yale University Press.

Elias, Norbert. 1978. *What Is Sociology?* Translated by Stephen Mennell and Grace Morrissey. New York: Columbia University Press.

Emirbayer, Mustafa. 1997. "Manifesto for a Relational Sociology." *American Journal of Sociology* 103, no. 2: 281–317. https://doi.org/10.1086/231209.

Feld, Scott L. 1991. "Why Your Friends Have More Friends Than You Do." *American Journal of Sociology* 96, 6: 1464–1477. https://doi.org/10.1086/229693.

Frier, Sarah. 2020. *No Filter: The Inside Story of Instagram*. New York: Simon & Schuster.

Gillespie, Tarleton. 2018. *Custodians of the Internet*. New Haven, CT: Yale University Press.

Holla, Sylvia. 2015. "Justifying Aesthetic Labor." *Journal of Contemporary Ethnography* 45, 4: 474–500. https://doi.org/10.1177/0891241615575067.

Maddox, Alexia. 2017. "Beyond Digital Dualism: Modeling Digital Community." In *Digital Sociologies*, edited by Jesse Daniels, Karen Gregory, and Tressie McMillan Cottom, 9–25. Bristol: Policy Press.

Marwick, Alice E. 2021. "Morally Motivated Networked Harassment as Normative Reinforcement." *Social Media + Society* 7, no. 2. https://doi.org/10.1177/20563051211021378.

Marwick, Alice E. 2013. *Status Update: Celebrity, Publicity, and Branding in the Social Media Age*. New Haven, CT: Yale University Press.

McNeil, Joanne. 2020. *Lurking: How a Person Became a User*. New York: MCD.

Miller, Daniel, Elisabetta Costa, Nell Haynes, Tom McDonald, Razvan Nicolescu, Jolynna Sinanan, et al. 2016. *How the World Changed Social Media*. London: UCL Press.

Orlowski, Jeff, dir. 2020. *The Social Dilemma*. Netflix.

Papacharissi, Zizi. 2014. *Affective Publics: Sentiment, Technology, and Politics*. New York: Oxford University Press.

Robinson, Jennifer. 2013. *Ordinary Cities: Between Modernity and Development*. London: Routledge.

Roy, Ananya. 2016. "Who's Afraid of Postcolonial Theory?" *International Journal of Urban and Regional Research* 40, no. 1: 200–209. https://doi.org/10.1111/1468-2427.12274.

Sobieraj, Sarah. 2020. *Credible Threat: Attacks Against Women Online and the Future of Democracy*. New York: Oxford University Press.

Thornton, Sarah. 2016. "Instagram's Mike Krieger Is a Game Changer." *Cultured Magazine*, May. https://www.culturedmag.com/article/2016/05/26/mike-krieger-instagram.

Törnberg, Petter, Christian Andersson, Kristian Lindgren, and Sven Banisch. 2021. "Modeling the Emergence of Affective Polarization in the Social Media Society." *PLOS ONE* 16, no. 10: 0258259. https://doi.org/10.1371/journal.pone.0258259.

Törnberg, Petter, and Justus Uitermark. 2021. "For a Heterodox Computational Social Science." *Big Data & Society* 8, no. 2: 1–13. https://doi.org/10.1177/20539517211047725.

Uitermark, Justus. 2009. "An *In Memoriam* for the Just City of Amsterdam." *City* 13, no. 2–3: 347–361. https://doi.org/10.1080/13604810902982813.

Uitermark, Justus, and Michiel van Meeteren. 2021. "Geographical Network Analysis." *Tijdschrift voor Economische en Sociale Geografie* 112, no. 4: 337–350. https://doi.org/10.1111/tesg.12480.

Valkenburg, Patti M., Adrian Meier, and Ine Beyens. 2022. "Social Media Use and Its Impact on Adolescent Mental Health: An Umbrella Review of the Evidence." *Current Opinion in Psychology* 44: 58–68. https://doi.org/10.1016/j.copsyc.2021.08.017.

Valkenburg, Patti M., and Jessica Taylor Piotrowski. 2017. *Plugged In: How Media Attract and Affect Youth.* New Haven, CT: Yale University Press.

van Dijck, José. 2013. *The Culture of Connectivity: A Critical History of Social Media.* New York: Oxford University Press.

Watts, Duncan J. 2011. *Everything Is Obvious: How Common Sense Fails Us.* New York: Crown.

Wellman, Barry, Anabel Quan-Haase, Jeffrey Boase, Wenchong Chen, Keith Hampton, Isabel Díaz, et al. 2003. "The Social Affordances of the Internet for Networked Individualism." *Journal of Computer-Mediated Communication* 8, no. 3. https://doi.org/10.1111/j.1083-6101.2003.tb00216.x.

Wells, Georgia, Jeff Horwitz, and Deepa Seetharaman. 2021. "Facebook Knows Instagram Is Toxic for Teen Girls, Company Documents Show." *Wall Street Journal*, September. https://www.wsj.com/articles/facebook-knows-instagram-is-toxic-for-teen-girls-company-documents-show-11631620739.

Wissinger, Elizabeth. 2015. *This Year's Model: Fashion, Media, and the Making of Glamour.* New York: NYU Press.

Zukin, Sharon. 1995. *The Cultures of Cities.* Oxford: Wiley.

Appendix

Blondel, Vincent D., Jean-Loup Guillaume, Renaud Lambiotte, and Etienne Lefebvre. 2008. "Fast Unfolding of Communities in Large Networks." *Journal of Statistical Mechanics: Theory and Experiment* 10: 10008. https://doi.org/10.1088/1742-5468/2008/10/p10008.

Boy, John D. 2015. *Kijkeens.* Zenodo. https://doi.org/10.5281/zenodo.34500.

Boy, John D., and Justus Uitermark. 2017. "Reassembling the City Through Instagram." *Transactions of the Institute of British Geographers* 42, no. 2: 612–624. https://doi.org/10.1111/tran.12185.

Boy, John D., and Justus Uitermark. 2020. "Lifestyle Enclaves in the Instagram City?" *Social Media+ Society* 6, no. 3: 2056305120940698.

Bronsvoort, Irene, and Justus L. Uitermark. 2022. "Seeing the Street Through Instagram: Digital Platforms and the Amplification of Gentrification." *Urban Studies* 59, no. 14: 2857–2874. https://doi.org/10.1177/00420980211046539.

Csardi, Gabor, and Tamas Nepusz. 2006. "The Igraph Software Package for Complex Network Research." *InterJournal: Complex Systems* 1695: 1–10.

Freelon, Deen. 2018. "Computational Research in the Post-API Age." *Political Communication* 35, no. 4: 665–668. https://doi.org/10.1080/10584609.2018.1477506.

Gillies, Sean. 2013. "The Shapely User Manual." https://shapely.readthedocs.io/.

Kluyver, Thomas, Benjamin Ragan-Kelley, Fernando Pérez, Brian Granger, Matthias Bussonnier, Jonathan Frederic, et al. 2016. "Jupyter Notebooks: A Publishing Format for Reproducible Computational Workflows." In *Positioning and Power in Academic Publishing: Players, Agents and Agendas. Proceedings of the 20th International Conference on Electronic Publishing*, edited by Fernando Loizides and Birgit Schmidt, 87–90. Amsterdam: IOS Press. https://doi.org/10.3233/978-1-61499-649-1-87.

Nelson, Laura K. 2020. "Computational Grounded Theory: A Methodological Framework." *Sociological Research & Methods* 49, no. 1: 3–42. https://doi.org/10.1177/0049124117729703.

Pardo-Guerra, Juan Pablo, and Prithviraj Pahwa. 2022. "The Extended Computational Case Method: A Framework for Research Design." *Sociological Methods & Research* 51, no. 4: 1826–1867. https://doi.org/10.1177/00491241221122616.

Savolainen, Laura, Justus Uitermark, and John D. Boy. 2022. "Filtering Feminisms: Emergent Feminist Visibilities on Instagram." *New Media & Society* 24, no. 3: 557–579. https://doi.org/10.1177/1461444820960074.

Whitaker, Jeffrey. 2016. "Pyproj Documentation." https://pyproj4.github.io/pyproj/.

Index

For the benefit of digital users, indexed terms that span two pages (e.g., 52–53) may, on occasion, appear on only one of those pages.
Tables are indicated by *t* following the page number

The manufacturer's authorised representative in the EU for product safety is Oxford University Press España S.A. of El Parque Empresarial San Fernando de Henares, Avenida de Castilla, 2 – 28830 Madrid (www.oup.es/en or product.safety@oup.com). OUP España S.A. also acts as importer into Spain of products made by the manufacturer.

Printed in the USA/Agawam, MA
August 15, 2025

892047.004